THE MEDITERRANEAN DIET ❤SEAFOOD LOVERS❤

This document is geared towards providing exact and reliable information in regards to the topic and issue covered. The publication is sold with the idea that the publisher is not required to render accounting, officially permitted, or otherwise, qualified services. If advice is necessary, legal or professional, a practiced individual in the profession should be ordered. From a Declaration of Principles which was accepted and approved equally by a Committee of the American bar association and a Committee of Publishersand Associations.In no way is it legal to reproduce, duplicate, or transmit any part of this document in either electronic means or in printed format. Recording of this publication is strictly prohibited and any storage of this document is not allowed unless with written permission from the publisher. All rights reserved. The information provided herein is stated to be truthful and consistent, in that any liability, in terms of inattention or otherwise, by any usage or abuse of any policies, processes, or directions contained within is the solitary and user responsibility of the recipient reader. Under no circumstances will any legal responsibility or blame be held against the publisher for any reparation, damages, or monetary loss due to the information herein, either directly or indirectly. Respective authors own all copyrights not held by the publisher. The information herein is offered for informational purposes solely and is universal as so. The presentation of the information is without contract or any type of guarantee assurance. The

trademarks that are used are without any consent, and the publication of the trademark is without permission or backing by the trademark owner. All trademarks and brands within this book are for clarifying purposes only and are the owned by the owners themselves, not affiliated with this document. The material in this book is for informational purposes only. As each individual situation is unique, you should use proper discretion, in consultation with healthcare practitioner, before undertaking the protocols, diet, exercises, techniques, training methods, or otherwise described herein. The author and publisher expressly disclaim responsibility for any adverse effects that may result fromtheuseor application of the information contained herein.

Recipes

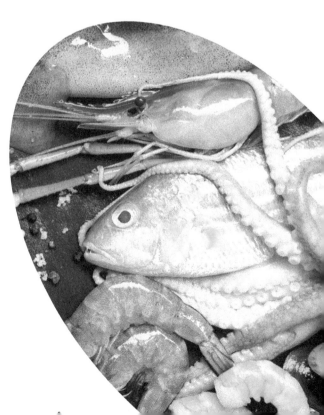

PREPARATION
40 MIN

SERVES FOR
4 PEOPLE

Roasted Salmon with Smoky Chickpeas & Greens

NUTRITION FACTS

Per Serving:
447 calories; protein 37g; carbohydrates 23.4g; fat 21.8g; cholesterol 72.9mg; sodium 556.7mg

INGREDIENTS

1/4 cup water
1/4 cup mayonnaise
1/4 cup chopped fresh chives and dill, plus more for garnish
1/4 teaspoon garlic powder
1/3 cup buttermilk
1/2 teaspoon salt, divided, plus a pinch
1/2 teaspoon ground pepper, divided
1 tablespoon smoked paprika
1 1/4 pounds wild salmon, cut into 4 portions
2 tablespoons extra-virgin olive oil, divided
10 cups chopped kale
15 ounce no-salt-added chickpeas, rinsed

STEPS

1. Position racks in upper third and middle of oven; preheat to 420 degrees F.
2. Place 1/4 teaspoon salt, 1 tablespoon oil, and paprika in a bowl. Very thoroughly pat chickpeas dry, then toss with the paprika mixture. Spread on a rimmed baking sheet. Bake the chickpeas on the upper rack, stirring twice, for 25 minutes.
3. Meanwhile, put mayonnaise, 1/4 teaspoon pepper, garlic powder puree buttermilk and herbs, in a blender until smooth. Set aside.
4. Heat the remaining 1 tablespoon oil in a skillet over medium heat. Add kale and cook, stirring occasionally, for 3 minutes. Add water and continue cooking for 4 minutes more. Remove from heat and stir in a pinch of salt.
5. Remove the chickpeas from the oven and push them to one side of the pan. Place salmon on the other side and season with the remaining 1/4 teaspoon each salt and pepper. Bake until the salmon is firm for around 9 minutes.
6. Drizzle the reserved dressing over the salmon, garnish with more herbs, and serve with kale and chickpeas.

Mediterranean Cod with Roasted Tomatoes

PREPARATION
5 MIN

SERVES FOR
4 PEOPLE

INGREDIENTS

1/4 teaspoon garlic powder
1/4 teaspoon paprika
1/4 teaspoon black pepper
1/2 teaspoon salt
1 teaspoon snipped fresh thyme
1 tablespoon olive oil
2 cloves garlic, sliced
2 tablespoons sliced pitted ripe olives
2 teaspoons capers
2 teaspoons snipped fresh oregano
3 cups cherry tomatoes
4 ounce fresh skinless cod fillets
Nonstick cooking spray
Fresh oregano

STEPS

1. Line a baking pan with foil. Coat foil with cooking spray.
2. Preheat oven to 450 degrees F. Rinse fish and pat dry with paper towels. In a bowl combine salt, garlic powder, paprika, snipped oregano, and black pepper. Sprinkle half of the oregano mixture over both sides of each fish fillet.
3. Place fish on one side of the foil-lined pan. Add tomatoes and garlic slices to the other side of the foil-lined pan. Combine the remaining oregano mixture with oil. Drizzle oil mixture over tomatoes. Bake for 13 minutes, stirring the tomato mixture. Add olives and capers into the cooked tomato mixture.
4. Divide the fish and roasted tomato mixture evenly among four serving plates. Garnish with fresh oregano. Serve!

NUTRITION FACTS

Per Serving:

157 calories
protein 21g
carbohydrates 6.5g
fat 4.8g
cholesterol 48.8mg
sodium 429.2mg

Linguine with Creamy White Clam Sauce

PREPARATION
15 MIN

SERVES FOR
4 PEOPLE

INGREDIENTS

1/4 cup chopped fresh basil, plus more for garnish
1/4 teaspoon crushed red pepper
1/4 teaspoon salt
1 tablespoon lemon juice
1 large tomato, chopped
2 tablespoons heavy cream
3 tablespoons extra-virgin olive oil
3 cloves garlic, chopped
8 ounces whole-wheat linguine
16 ounce clams baby

NUTRITION FACTS

Per Serving:

421 calories
protein 21.5g
carbohydrates 51.9g
fat 16.9g
cholesterol: 48.2mg
sodium: 371.9mg

STEPS

1. Bring a saucepan of water to the a boil. Add pasta and cook, for 8 minutes or according to package directions. Drain.
2. Meanwhile, drain the clams, reserving 3/4 cup of the liquid. Heat oil in a skillet over medium heat. Add garlic and crushed red pepper and cook, stirring, for 40 seconds. Add the reserved clam liquid, lemon juice, and salt; bring to a simmer and cook until slightly reduced for 3 minutes. Add the tomato and clams; bring to a simmer and cook for 1 minute more. Remove from heat.
3. Stir in basil and cream. Add the pasta and toss to coat with the sauce. Garnish with more basil and serve!

Salmon with Roasted Red Pepper Quinoa

PREPARATION
15 MIN

SERVES FOR
4 PEOPLE

INGREDIENTS

1/4 cup chopped fresh cilantro
1/4 cup chopped toasted pistachios
1/2 teaspoon salt, divided
1/2 teaspoon ground pepper, divided
1 clove garlic, grated
1 cup chopped roasted red bell peppers rinsed
1 1/4 pounds skin-on salmon, preferably wild, cut into 4 portions
2 tablespoons red-wine vinegar
2 cups cooked quinoa
3 tablespoons extra-virgin olive oil, divided

STEPS

1. Heat 1 tablespoon oil in a nonstick skillet over medium heat. Pat the salmon dry and sprinkle the flesh with 1/4 teaspoon each salt and pepper. Add to the pan, skin-side up, and cook for 6 minutes. Transfer to a plate.
2. Meanwhile, add the remaining 2 tablespoons of oil, vinegar, garlic, 1/4 teaspoon each salt and pepper, in a bowl. Add quinoa, peppers, cilantro, and pistachios; toss to combine. Serve!

NUTRITION FACTS

Per Serving:

481 calories
protein 35.8g
carbohydrates 31g
fat 21g
cholesterol 66.3mg
sodium 707mg

Beet & Shrimp Winter Salad

PREPARATION
15 MIN

SERVES FOR
1 PEOPLE

INGREDIENTS

Vinaigrette
1/8 teaspoon salt
1/4 teaspoon ground pepper
1/2 teaspoon Dijon mustard
1/2 teaspoon minced shallot
1 tablespoon red wine vinegar
2 tablespoons extra-virgin olive oil
Salad
1/2 cup zucchini ribbons
1/2 cup thinly sliced fennel
1/2 cup cooked barley
1 cup watercress
1 cup cooked beet wedges
2 cups lightly packed arugula
4 ounces cooked, peeled shrimp
Fennel fronds for garnish

STEPS

1. Arrange watercress, beets, zucchini, fennel, arugula, barley, and shrimp on a dinner plate.
2. Whisk vinegar, oil, mustard, shallot, pepper, and salt in a bowl, then drizzle over the salad. Garnish with fennel fronds. Serve!

NUTRITION FACTS

Per Serving:

584 calories
protein 35g
carbohydrates 47g
fat 29.8g
cholesterol 214mg
sodium 653mg

Farfalle with Tuna, Lemon, and Fennel

PREPARATION
5 MIN

SERVES FOR
4 PEOPLE

INGREDIENTS

1/4 teaspoon salt
1/2 teaspoon crushed red pepper
1 Olive oil
1 cup fennel, thinly sliced
1 teaspoon lemon peel, finely shredded
2 cloves garlic, minced
2 tablespoons snipped fresh parsley
5 ounce can solid white tuna (packed in oil)
6 ounces dried whole grain farfalle pasta
14.5 ounce no-salt-added diced tomatoes, undrained

STEPS

1. Cook pasta according to package directions, with salt; drain. Return pasta to pan; cover and keep warm. Meanwhile, drain tuna, reserving oil.
2. In a saucepan heat the 3 tablespoons of reserved oil over medium heat. Add fennel; cook for 4 minutes, stirring. Add garlic, crushed red pepper, and salt; cook and stir for about 1 minute. Stir in tomatoes. Bring to boiling; reduce heat. Simmer, uncovered, for 7 minutes. Stir in tuna; simmer, uncovered, about 1 minute more.
3. Pour tuna mixture over pasta; stir to combine. Garnish each serving with parsley and lemon peel. Serve!

NUTRITION FACTS

Per Serving:

356 calories
protein 16.7g
carbohydrates 42.8g
fat 14.2g
cholesterol 11mg
sodium 380mg

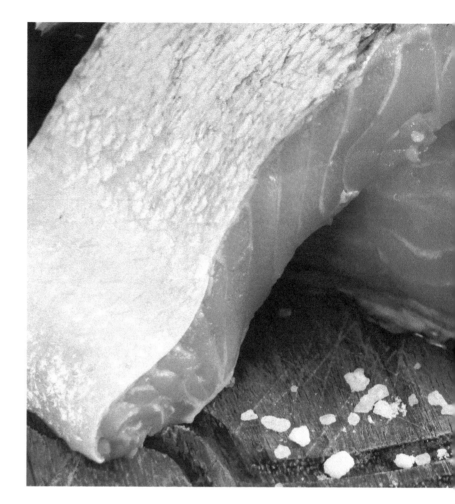

PREPARATION
15MIN

SERVES FOR
4 PEOPLE

Creamy Salmon & Sugar Snap Cauliflower Gnocchi

NUTRITION FACTS

Per Serving:
194 calories; protein 9.3g; carbohydrates 18g; fat 8.3g; cholesterol 21.9mg; sodium 240mg

INGREDIENTS

2 tablespoons low-fat plain Greek yogurt
2 tablespoons water
3/4 pound sugar snap peas, trimmed
4 tablespoons cream cheese, cubed
4 ounces flaked smoked salmon
12 ounce bag frozen cauliflower gnocchi
Freshly ground pepper to taste

STEPS

1. Cook gnocchi according to package directions.
2. Place peas in a microwave-safe baking dish and add water. Cover tightly and microwave on High, about 3 minutes.
3. Heat cream cheese in a nonstick skillet just until melted. Add the gnocchi, yogurt, and peas. Stir to coat. Top with salmon and a sprinkle of pepper. Serve!

Seared Salmon with Pesto Fettuccine

PREPARATION
20 MIN

SERVES FOR
4 PEOPLE

INGREDIENTS

1/4 teaspoon salt
1/4 teaspoon ground pepper
1 tablespoon extra-virgin olive oil
1 1/4 pounds wild salmon, skinned and cut into 4 portions
2/3 cup pesto
8 ounces whole-wheat fettuccine

STEPS

1. Bring a pot of water to a boil. Add fettuccine and cook for about 10 minutes. Drain and transfer to a bowl. Toss with pesto.
2. Meanwhile, season salmon with pepper and salt. Heat oil in a cast-iron skillet over medium heat. Add salmon and cook, turning once, for 3 minutes per side. Add the salmon to the pasta and jumbled up. Serve!

NUTRITION FACTS

Per Serving:

603 calories
protein 44g
carbohydrates 45g
fat 28g
cholesterol 79.6mg
sodium 537mg

Quick Shrimp

PREPARATION
15 MIN

SERVES FOR
4 PEOPLE

INGREDIENTS

1/4 teaspoon salt
1/4 cup chopped pitted olives
1 tablespoon capers, rinsed
1 tablespoon extra-virgin olive oil
1 pound peeled and deveined large shrimp
8 ounces refrigerated fresh linguine noodles, preferably whole-wheat
8 ounces frozen quartered artichoke hearts, thawed
15 ounce no-salt-added tomato sauce

STEPS

1. Bring a pot of water to a boil. Cook linguine according to package instructions. Drain.
2. Meanwhile, heat oil in a skillet over high heat. Add shrimp in a single layer and cook, for 3 minutes. Stir in tomato sauce. Add olives, capers, artichoke hearts, and salt; cook, stirring often, for 3 minutes longer.
3. Add the drained noodles to the sauce and stir to combine. Divide among 4 pasta portions. Serve.

NUTRITION FACTS

Per Serving:

390 calories;
protein 36.7g
carbohydrates 43.4g
fat 8g
cholesterol 241mg
sodium 629mg

Shrimp with Cauliflower Gnocchi

PREPARATION
15 MIN

SERVES FOR
4 PEOPLE

INGREDIENTS

1/4 teaspoon oregano
1 pint grape tomatoes, halved
1 tablespoon olive oil
1 pound cooked peeled shrimp
2 teaspoons minced garlic
12 ounce bag frozen cauliflower gnocchi
Pinch of salt

STEPS

1. Cook gnocchi according to package directions.
2. Combine tomatoes, oil, garlic, oregano, and salt in a microwave-safe bowl. Microwave on High, about 1 minute. Stir in the gnocchi and shrimp. Serve!

NUTRITION FACTS

Per Serving:

133calories
protein 2g
carbohydrates 16.8g
fat 5.5g
sodium 40.3mg

Sheet-Pan Shrimp & Beets

PREPARATION
15 MIN

SERVES FOR
4 PEOPLE

INGREDIENTS

1/2 teaspoon dry mustard
1/2 teaspoon dried tarragon
1 pound small beets
1 1/4 pounds extra-large raw shrimp, peeled and deveined
2 tablespoons extra-virgin olive oil, divided
3 tablespoons unsalted sunflower seeds, toasted
3/4 teaspoon salt, divided
3/4 teaspoon ground pepper, divided
6 cups chopped kale

NUTRITION FACTS

Per Serving:

266calories
protein 28.9g
carbohydrates 14.8g
fat 11.1g
cholesterol 198mg
sodium 680mg

STEPS

1. Preheat oven to 435 F.
2. Toss beets with 1 tablespoon oil and 1/4 teaspoon each salt and pepper in a bowl. Spread evenly on a rimmed baking sheet. Roast for 16 minutes.
3. Toss kale with the remaining 1 tablespoon oil and 1/4 teaspoon each salt and pepper in the bowl. Stir into the beets on the baking sheet.
4. Sprinkle shrimp with mustard, tarragon, and the remaining 1/4 teaspoon of each salt and pepper. Place on top of the vegetables. Roast until the shrimp are cooked and the vegetables are tender, for 15 minutes more.
5. Transfer the shrimp to a serving platter. Stir sunflower seeds into the vegetables and serve with the shrimp.

Salmon & Asparagus with Lemon-Garlic Butter Sauce

PREPARATION
10 MIN

SERVES FOR
4 PEOPLE

INGREDIENTS

1/2 teaspoon salt
1/2 teaspoon ground pepper
1/2 tablespoon grated garlic
1 pound center-cut salmon fillet, preferably wild, cut into 4 portions
1 tablespoon extra-virgin olive oil
1 teaspoon grated lemon zest
1 tablespoon lemon juice
1 pound fresh asparagus, trimmed
3 tablespoons butter

STEPS

1. Coat a large rimmed baking sheet with cooking spray.
2. Preheat oven to 400 degrees F.
3. Place salmon on one side of the prepared baking sheet and asparagus on the other. Sprinkle the salmon and asparagus with salt and pepper.
4. Heat oil, butter, garlic, lemon zest, and lemon juice in a skillet over medium heat until the butter is melted. Drizzle the butter mixture over the salmon and asparagus. Bake and cook for 14 minutes. Serve!

NUTRITION FACTS

Per Serving:

270 calories
protein 25.4g
carbohydrates 5.6g
fat 16.5g
cholesterol 75mg
sodium 350.5mg

Roasted Cod with Warm Tomato-Olive-Caper Tapenade

PREPARATION
25 MIN

SERVES FOR
4 PEOPLE

INGREDIENTS

1/4 cup chopped cured olives
1/4 teaspoon freshly ground pepper
1 pound cod fillet
1 teaspoon balsamic vinegar
1 tablespoon minced shallot
1 cup halved cherry tomatoes
1 tablespoon capers, rinsed and chopped
1 1/2 teaspoons chopped fresh oregano
3 teaspoons extra-virgin olive oil, divided

STEPS

1. Coat a baking sheet with cooking spray.
2. Preheat oven to 450F.
3. Rub cod with 2 teaspoons of oil and sprinkle with pepper. Place on the prepared baking sheet. Transfer to the oven and roast for 20 minutes.
4. Meanwhile, heat the remaining 1 teaspoon oil in a skillet over medium heat, add shallot, and cook, stirring, until beginning to soften. Add tomatoes and cook, stirring, until softened, about 10 minutes. Add olives and capers; cook, stirring, for 40 seconds more. Stir in oregano and vinegar; remove from heat. Spoon the tapenade over the cod to serve.

NUTRITION FACTS

Per Serving:

151 calories
protein 15.4g
carbohydrates 3.9g
fat 8g
cholesterol 44.6mg
sodium 588mg

Seared Cod with Spinach-Lemon Sauce

PREPARATION
25 MIN

SERVES FOR
4 PEOPLE

INGREDIENTS

1/4 teaspoon crushed red pepper
1/4 cup sliced toasted almonds
1/2 teaspoon salt, divided
1/2 teaspoon ground pepper, divided
1/2cup lightly packed fresh parsley sprigs
1 clove garlic, quartered
1 tablespoon grapeseed oil
1 1/4 pounds cod , cut into 4 portions
1 5-ounce package baby spinach
3 tablespoons water
4 teaspoons lemon juice
4 teaspoons orange juice

NUTRITION FACTS

Per Serving:

163 calories
protein 20.9g
carbohydrates 4.4g
fat 7g
cholesterol 55.8mg
sodium 393mg

STEPS

1. Place spinach and water in a microwave-safe bowl. Cover with plastic wrap and poke a few holes in it. Microwave on High until wilted, about 2 minutes.
2. Puree the wilted spinach and any remaining water, lemon juice, orange juice, garlic, 1/4 teaspoon each salt, pepper, and crushed red pepper parsley, in a blender until smooth. Set aside.
3. Sprinkle cod with the remaining 1/4 teaspoon of each salt and pepper.
4. Heat oil in a nonstick skillet over medium heat. Cook the cod, turning once, for 8 minutes total. Transfer to a plate.
5. Pour the reserved sauce into the pan and cook, stirring occasionally, for about 2 minutes. Serve the fish on top of the sauce, sprinkled with almonds.

Mediterranean Shrimp and Pasta

PREPARATION
25 MIN

SERVES FOR
4 PEOPLE

INGREDIENTS

1/4 cup chopped fresh basil
1/4 teaspoon salt
1/2 cup dry white wine
1 cup sliced zucchini
1 cup red sweet pepper, chopped
1 tablespoon olive oil
1 1/2 teaspoons chopped fresh rosemary
2 ounces reduced-fat feta cheese, crumbled
2 cloves garlic, minced
4 ounces dried acini di pepe
8 ounces fresh medium shrimp
8 pitted olives, coarsely chopped
14.5 ounce no-salt-added diced tomatoes, drained
Nonstick cooking spray

STEPS

1. Peel shrimp and cover. Lightly coat an unheated 1 1/2-quart slow cooker with cooking spray. In the slow cooker combine tomatoes, zucchini, garlic, sweet pepper, and wine.
2. Cover and cook on a low-heat setting for 3/3: 30 hours. Stir in the shrimp. Cook for 30 minutes more.
3. Combine olive oil, olives, basil, rosemary, and salt. Place cooked pasta in a serving bowl and top with shrimp mixture. Sprinkle feta cheese evenly overall. Serve!

NUTRITION FACTS

Per Serving:

302 calories
protein 19.9g
carbohydrates 32.4g
fat 8g
cholesterol 90.3mg
sodium 571mg

PREPARATION
1 HOUR

SERVES FOR
4 PEOPLE

Caramelized Onion, Olive & Anchovy

NUTRITION FACTS

Per Serving:
230 calories; protein 6.5g; carbohydrates 26.6g; fat 10.9g; cholesterol 5.1mg; sodium 286.2mg

INGREDIENTS

1/4 teaspoon ground black pepper
1/2 teaspoon salt
1 cup chickpea flour
1 medium onion, thinly sliced
1 cup water
2 teaspoons chopped fresh thyme
3 tablespoons extra-virgin olive oil, divided
6 anchovies
8 oil-cured olives, pitted and halved

STEPS

1. Preheat to 450 degrees F.
2. Whisk flour, salt, and pepper in a bowl. Add water; whisk until smooth. Let rest while the oven preheats.
3. Place a cast-iron skillet on the lower rack.
4. Meanwhile, heat 1 tablespoon oil in a skillet over medium heat. Add onion and cook, stirring occasionally, for about 12 minutes, adding a tablespoon or two of water, if needed.
5. When the oven is preheated, carefully remove the hot pan and swirl in 1 tablespoon oil. Whisk the batter, pour it into the pan and swirl to coat. Top with the onion, anchovies, and olives.
6. Bake until the bottom is browned and the edges are crispy, for 20 minutes. Remove from the oven and, using a pastry brush, dab the socca with the remaining 1 tablespoon oil.
7. Turn the broiler too high. Broil the socca on the upper rack until browned in spots, 2 to 3 minutes. Garnish with thyme and cut into wedges.
8. Serve!

Grilled Mediterranean Salmon in Foil

PREPARATION
15 MIN

SERVES FOR
4 PEOPLE

INGREDIENTS

1/2 teaspoon salt
1 small shallot, finely chopped
2 tablespoons black olive tapenade
4 tablespoons extra-virgin olive oil
4 small fresh thyme sprigs
4 pieces aluminum foil
7 ounce salmon filets, with skin
10 ounce basket cherry tomatoes, quartered
Freshly ground black pepper to taste

NUTRITION FACTS

Per Serving:

493 calories
protein 36.2g
carbohydrates 9.5g
fat 34.4g
cholesterol 97.8mg
sodium 458mg

STEPS

1. Preheat an outdoor grill for high heat and lightly oil the grate. Close cover.
2. Combine olive oil, tapenade, salt, basil, thyme, cherry tomatoes, shallot, and pepper in a bowl; mix well.
3. Lay out foil on a work surface, shiny side-up. Place each salmon fillet skin-side-down in the center of a piece of foil. Cover each piece of salmon with 1/4 of the cherry tomato mixture. Fold up the edges of the foil over the salmon to create a parcel, making sure to seal the edges well.
4. Turn down the heat of the grill and carefully place the foil parcels on the grate. Close the cover and cook for 8 minutes. Remove parcels and let them sit for a few minutes before opening.
5. Serve!

Pan-Seared Scallops
with Pepper and Onions
in Anchovy Oil

PREPARATION
30 MIN

SERVES FOR
4 PEOPLE

INGREDIENTS

1/2 cup extra virgin olive oil
1 pinch salt and pepper to taste
1 teaspoon minced lime zest
1 pound large sea scallops
1 large red bell pepper, coarsely chopped
1 large orange bell pepper, coarsely chopped
1 red onion, coarsely chopped
1 1/2 teaspoons minced lemon zest
2 ounce anchovy fillets, minced
2 cloves garlic, thinly sliced
8 sprigs fresh parsley, for garnish

STEPS

1. Heat the olive oil and minced anchovies in a skillet over medium-high heat, stirring as the oil heats to dissolve the anchovies. Once the anchovies are sizzling, add the sea scallops, and cook without moving the scallops for 2 minutes.
2. Meanwhile, toss orange bell pepper, red bell pepper, garlic,
3. red onion, lime zest, and lemon zest in a bowl. Season with salt and pepper. Sprinkle pepper mixture onto the scallops and continue cooking for 3 minutes more. Turn scallops, stir the pepper mixture, and continue cooking until the scallops have browned on the other side, for 5 minutes. Garnish with parsley sprigs to serve.

NUTRITION FACTS

Per Serving:

368 calories
protein 24.2g
carbohydrates 14.4g
fat 23.9g
cholesterol 45mg
sodium 752mg

Swordfish with Olives, Capers & Tomatoes over Polenta

PREPARATION
20 MIN

SERVES FOR
4 PEOPLE

INGREDIENTS

1/8 teaspoon ground pepper
1/4 cup green olives rinsed, pitted, and coarsely chopped
1/2 teaspoon salt, divided
1/2 cup coarse or regular yellow cornmeal or polenta
1 pound swordfish, cut into 4 steaks
1 tablespoon capers, rinsed
1 tablespoon extra-virgin olive oil
2 cloves garlic, minced
2 1/2 cups water
3 tablespoons chopped fresh basil
4 medium stalks celery, diced
15 ounce no-salt-added diced tomatoes
Pinch of crushed red pepper
Fresh basil for garnish

NUTRITION FACTS

Per Serving:

276 calories
protein 22.1g
carbohydrates 18.9g
fat 12.1g
cholesterol 64.6mg
sodium 536mg

STEPS

1. Bring 2 cups of water to a boil in a saucepan over high heat. Add 1/4 tsp. salt. Slowly pour in cornmeal in a gentle stream, stirring rapidly with a whisk to avoid lumps. Cook, stirring until the mixture starts to thicken, about 4 minutes.
2. Reduce heat to a low simmer. Cook, stirring every 4 minutes until the polenta easily comes away from the sides of the pan, for about 25 minutes. Remove from heat and cover.
3. Meanwhile, heat oil in a skillet over medium heat. Add celery; cook, stirring occasionally, for about 6 minutes. Add garlic; cook for 40 seconds. Stir in tomatoes, olives, capers, crushed red pepper, basil, ground pepper, and the remaining 1/4 tsp. salt. Cover, reduce heat to low and simmer for 6 minutes.
4. Place swordfish steaks in the simmering sauce. Cover and cook until the fish is cooked through, about 15 minutes.
5. To serve, spoon the polenta onto a large serving platter. Arrange the fish over the polenta, top with the sauce, and garnish with fresh basil.
6. Serve!

Fish Stew

PREPARATION
25 MIN

SERVES FOR
2 PEOPLE

INGREDIENTS

1/4 cup sliced green onions
1/2 tablespoon chopped fresh basil
1/2 tablespoon chopped fresh oregano
1 pinch minced fresh rosemary
1 cup clam juice
1 pound shrimp, peeled and deveined
1 tablespoon chopped fresh parsley
1 anchovy fillet
2 pinches red pepper flakes
3 cups cherry tomatoes, halved
4 tablespoons olive oil, divided
4 cloves garlic, sliced
12 ounces halibut
Salt to taste

NUTRITION FACTS

Per Serving:

672 calories
protein 76.3g
carbohydrates 14.3g
fat 34.1g
cholesterol 405mg
sodium 922mg

STEPS

1. Puree cherry tomatoes and clam juice in a blender until smooth. Press mixture through a fine-mesh strainer into a bowl.
2. Combine 3 tablespoons of olive oil, garlic,
3. green onions, anchovy, and 1 pinch of red pepper flakes in a cold plan. Place over medium heat. Cook and stir for about 4 minutes. Stir in the tomato mixture. Bring to a simmer over medium-high heat. Reduce heat to medium and simmer the stew for about 10 minutes.
4. Add halibut and shrimp to the stew. Season with salt. Increase heat to high. Cover the pan and cook for about 6 minutes. Stir in basil, parsley, oregano, and rosemary. Pour stew into a bowl. Shower in remaining olive oil and sprinkle 1 pinch of red pepper flakes on top. Serve!

Walnut-Rosemary Crusted Salmon

PREPARATION
10 MIN

SERVES FOR
4 PEOPLE

INGREDIENTS

1/4 teaspoon lemon zest
1/4 teaspoon crushed red pepper
1/2 teaspoon honey
1/2 teaspoon salt
1 teaspoon extra-virgin olive oil
1 pound skinless salmon fillet, fresh
1 clove garlic, minced
1 teaspoon lemon juice
1 teaspoon chopped fresh rosemary
2 teaspoons mustard
3 tablespoons panko breadcrumbs
3 tablespoons finely chopped walnuts
Olive oil cooking spray
Chopped fresh parsley and lemon wedges for garnish

STEPS

1. Line a rimmed baking sheet with parchment paper.
2. Preheat oven to 435 degrees F.
3. Combine lemon zest, lemon juice, mustard, honey, rosemary, garlic, salt, and crushed red pepper in a bowl. Combine oil, panko, and walnuts, in another bowl.
4. Place salmon on the prepared baking sheet. Spread the mustard mixture over the fish and sprinkle with the panko mixture. Lightly coat with cooking spray.
5. Bake for about 13 minutes.
6. Garnish with parsley and serve with lemon wedges.

NUTRITION FACTS

Per Serving:

222 calories
protein 24g
carbohydrates 4g
fat 12g
cholesterol 62mg
sodium 256mg

Shrimp & Pesto

INGREDIENTS

1/4 teaspoon ground pepper
1/2 teaspoon salt
1/2 cup prepared pesto
1 tablespoon extra-virgin olive oil
1 cup halved cherry tomatoes
1 avocado, diced
1 pound peeled and deveined shrimp patted dry
2 tablespoons balsamic vinegar
2 cups cooked quinoa
4 cups arugula

STEPS

1. Combine oil, pesto, vinegar, salt, and pepper in a bowl and stir. Remove 4 tablespoons of the mixture to a bowl; set both bowls aside.
2. Heat a cast-iron skillet over medium heat. Add shrimp and cook, stirring, for 5 minutes. Remove to a plate.
3. Add arugula and quinoa to the bowl with the vinaigrette and toss to coat. Divide the arugula mixture between 4 bowls. Top with avocado, tomatoes, and shrimp. Garnish each bowl with 1 tablespoon of the reserved pesto mixture.
4. Serve!

NUTRITION FACTS

Per Serving:

429 calories
protein 30.9g
carbohydrates 29.3g
fat 3.6g
cholesterol 187mg
sodium 571mg

Sheet-Pan Salmon with Sweet Potatoes & Broccoli

PREPARATION
30 MIN

SERVES FOR
4 PEOPLE

INGREDIENTS

1/4 teaspoon ground pepper, divided
1/4 cup crumbled feta cheese
1/2 teaspoon salt, divided
1/2 cup chopped fresh cilantro
1 teaspoon chili powder
1 1/4 pounds salmon fillet, cut into 4 portions
2 limes, 1 zested and juiced, 1 cut into wedges
for serving
2 medium sweet potatoes, peeled and cut
3 tablespoons low-fat mayonnaise
4 teaspoons olive oil, divided
4 cups broccoli florets

NUTRITION FACTS

Per Serving:

504 calories
protein 34g
carbohydrates 34g
fat 26g
cholesterol 83mg
sodium 642mg

STEPS

1. Line a rimmed baking sheet with foil and coat with cooking spray.
2. Preheat oven to 415 degrees F.
3. Combine chili powder and mayonnaise in a bowl. Set aside.
4. Toss sweet potatoes with 2 tsp. oil, 1/4 tsp. salt, and 1/8 tsp. pepper in a bowl. Spread on the prepared baking sheet. Roast for 16 minutes.
5. Meanwhile, toss broccoli with the remaining 2 tsp. oil, 1/4 tsp. salt, and 1/8 tsp. pepper in the same bowl. Remove the baking sheet from the oven. Stir the sweet potatoes and move them to the sides of the pan. Arrange salmon in the center of the pan and spread the broccoli on either side, among the sweet potatoes. Spread 2 Tbsp. of the mayonnaise mixture over the salmon. Bake until the sweet potatoes are tender about 17 minutes.
6. Meanwhile, add lime zest and lime juice to the remaining 1 Tbsp. mayonnaise; mix well.
7. Divide the salmon among 4 plates and garnish with cheese and cilantro. Divide the sweet potatoes and broccoli among the plates and drizzle with the lime-mayonnaise sauce. Serve with lime wedges and any remaining sauce.

PREPARATION
20 MIN

SERVES FOR
4 PEOPLE

BBQ Shrimp with Garlicky Kale & Parmesan-Herb Couscous

NUTRITION FACTS

Per Serving:
414 calories; protein 32.2g; carbohydrates 36.4g; fat 16.9g; cholesterol 195mg; sodium 606 mg

INGREDIENTS

1/4 cup water
1/4 teaspoon crushed red pepper
1/4 teaspoon salt
1/4 cup barbecue sauce
1/4 teaspoon poultry seasoning
1/3 cup grated Parmesan cheese
1 cup low-sodium chicken broth
1 tablespoon butter
1 large clove garlic, smashed
1 pound peeled and deveined raw shrimp
2/3 cup whole-wheat couscous
3 tablespoons extra-virgin olive oil, divided
8 cups chopped kale

STEPS

1. Combine broth and poultry seasoning in a saucepan over medium heat. Bring to a boil. Stir in couscous. Remove from heat, cover, and let stand for 10 minutes. Fluff with a fork, then stir in Parmesan and butter. Cover to keep warm.
2. Meanwhile, heat 1 tablespoon oil in a skillet over medium heat. Add kale and cook, stirring, for 2 minutes. Add water, cover, and cook, stirring occasionally, for about 4 minutes. Reduce heat to medium-low. Make a well in the center of the kale and add 1 tablespoon oil, garlic, and crushed red pepper; cook, for 20 seconds, then stir the garlic oil into the kale and season with salt. Transfer to a bowl and cover.
3. Add the remaining 1 tablespoon oil and shrimp to the pan. Cook, stirring for about 3 minutes. Remove from heat and stir in barbecue sauce. Serve the shrimp with kale and couscous.

One Salmon with Fennel

PREPARATION
30 MIN

SERVES FOR
4 PEOPLE

INGREDIENTS

1/4 cup sliced green olives
1/4 teaspoon salt
1/4 teaspoon ground pepper
1 cup couscous, preferably whole-wheat
1 lemon
1 1/4 pounds salmon, skinned and cut into 4 portions
1 1/2 cups low-sodium chicken broth
2 tablespoons toasted pine nuts
2 cloves garlic, sliced
2 tablespoons extra-virgin olive oil, divided
2 medium fennel bulbs, cut into
3 scallions, sliced
4 tablespoons sun-dried tomato pesto, divided

NUTRITION FACTS

Per Serving:

543 calories
protein 38.3g
carbohydrates 46g
fat 24g
cholesterol 67mg
sodium 440mg

STEPS

1. Zest lemon and reserve the zest. Cut the lemon into 8 slices. Season salmon with salt and pepper and spread 1 1/2 teaspoons pesto on each piece.
2. Heat 1 tablespoon oil in a skillet over medium heat. Add half the fennel; cook for 3 minutes. Transfer to a plate. Reduce heat and repeat with the remaining 1 tablespoon oil and fennel. Transfer to the plate. Add couscous and scallions to the pan; cook, stirring frequently, until the couscous is lightly toasted, for 2 minutes. Stir in broth, pine nuts, garlic, olives, the reserved lemon zest, and the remaining 2 tablespoons pesto.
3. Nestle the fennel and salmon into the couscous. Top the salmon with lemon slices. Reduce heat to low, cover, and cook about for 15 minutes. Garnish with fennel fronds.
4. Serve!

Sweet & Spicy Roasted Salmon with Wild Rice

PREPARATION
15 MIN

SERVES FOR
4 PEOPLE

INGREDIENTS

1/8 teaspoon ground pepper
1/4 cup chopped fresh parsley
1/4 teaspoon salt
1 small jalapeño pepper, seeded and finely chopped
1 tablespoon honey
1 cup chopped red bell pepper
2 tablespoons balsamic vinegar
2 scallions (green parts only), thinly sliced
2 2/3 cups Wild Rice Pilaf
5 skinless salmon fillets, fresh

STEPS

1. Preheat oven to 420 degrees F. Line a baking pan with parchment paper. Place the salmon in the prepared pan. Whisk vinegar and honey in a bowl; drizzle half of the mixture over the salmon. Sprinkle with salt and pepper.

2. Roast the salmon for about 15 minutes. Drizzle with the remaining vinegar mixture.

3. Coat a nonstick skillet with cooking spray; heat over medium heat. Add bell pepper and jalapeño; cook, stirring frequently, for 5 minutes. Remove from heat. Stir in scallion greens.

4. Top of the salmon fillets with the pepper mixture and parsley. Serve with pilaf.

NUTRITION FACTS

Per Serving:

339 calories
protein 29.6g
carbohydrates 42.5g
fat 5.3g
cholesterol 53mg
sodium 442mg

Roasted Pistachio-Crusted Salmon with Broccoli

PREPARATION
30 MIN

SERVES FOR
4 PEOPLE

INGREDIENTS

1/2 teaspoon ground pepper, divided
1/2 cup salted pistachios, coarsely chopped
1 1/4 pounds salmon fillet, cut into 4 portions
2 tablespoons chopped fresh chives
2 cloves garlic, sliced
3 tablespoons extra-virgin olive oil, divided
3/4 teaspoon salt, divided
4 teaspoons mayonnaise
8 cups broccoli florets with stalks attached
Zest of 1 medium lemon, plus wedges for serving

STEPS

1. Coat a rimmed baking sheet with cooking spray.
2. Preheat oven to 450 degrees F.
3. Combine 2 tablespoons of oil, garlic, broccoli, 1/2 teaspoon salt, and 1/4 teaspoon pepper on the prepared baking sheet. Roast for 6 minutes.
4. Meanwhile, combine pistachios, chives, lemon zest, the remaining 1 tablespoon oil, and 1/4 teaspoon each salt and pepper in a bowl. Spread 1 teaspoon mayonnaise over each salmon portion and top with the pistachio mixture.
5. Move the broccoli to one side of the baking sheet and place the salmon on the empty side. Roast until the salmon is opaque in the center and the broccoli for 15 minutes more, depending on thickness. Serve with lemon wedges.

NUTRITION FACTS

Per Serving:

424calories
protein 36g
carbohydrates 12.3g
fat 26.7g
cholesterol 68mg
sodium 639mg

One-Pot Pasta with Tuna

PREPARATION
35 MIN

SERVES FOR
4 PEOPLE

INGREDIENTS

1/2 teaspoon salt
1/2 teaspoon ground pepper
1/2 cup olives, cut away from the pit
2 tablespoons extra-virgin olive oil
2 teaspoons fresh lemon zest, plus juice of half
a lemon
3 tablespoons chopped fresh dill
3 1/4 cups water
5 ounce unsalted tuna, drained and flaked
8 ounces whole-wheat spaghetti

STEPS

1. Combine water, spaghetti, olives, lemon juice, lemon zest, salt, and pepper in a deep skillet. Bring to a boil, reduce heat to maintain a lively simmer, and cook, stirring occasionally, until most of the water is absorbed and the pasta is tender for 12 minutes. Remove from heat and stir in tuna, dill, and oil.
2. Serve!

NUTRITION FACTS

Per Serving:

382 calories
protein 21.7g
carbohydrates 42.2g
fat 15g
cholesterol 25.5mg
sodium 666.7mg

PREPARATION
30 MIN

SERVES FOR
4 PEOPLE

Shrimp Scampi Zoodles

NUTRITION FACTS

Per Serving:
286 calories; protein 27.4g; carbohydrates 8.1g; fat 15.4g; cholesterol 201mg; sodium 530mg

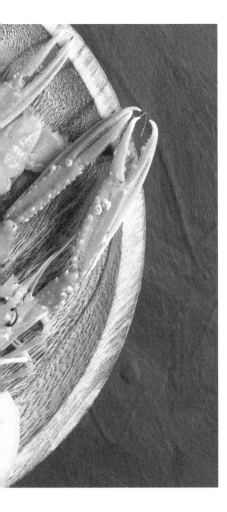

INGREDIENTS

1/4 cup chopped fresh parsley
1/4 teaspoon ground pepper
1/4 cup grated Parmesan cheese
1/2 teaspoon salt, divided
1/3 cup dry white wine
1 tablespoon minced garlic
1 pound peeled raw shrimp
1 tablespoon lemon juice
2 tablespoons butter
2 tablespoons extra-virgin olive oil, divided
6 medium zucchini, trimmed
Lemon wedges for serving

STEPS

1. Using a spiral vegetable slicer, cut zucchini lengthwise into long, thin strands or strips. Place the zucchini noodles in a colander and toss with 1/4 teaspoon salt. Let drain for 35 minutes, then gently squeeze to remove any excess liquid.
2. Meanwhile, heat butter and 1 tablespoon oil in a skillet over medium-high heat. Add garlic and cook, stirring, for 30 seconds. Carefully add wine and bring to a simmer. Add shrimp and cook, stirring, for 4 minutes. Remove from heat and add lemon juice, parsley, pepper, and the remaining 1/4 teaspoon salt; stir to combine. Transfer to a bowl and set aside.
3. Heat the remaining 1 tablespoon oil in the skillet over medium heat. Add zucchini and gently toss until hot, about 4 minutes. Pour the shrimp mixture over the zucchini and gently toss to combine. Serve sprinkled with Parmesan and a squeeze of lemon.

Garlic-Sautéed Shrimp

PREPARATION
40 MIN

SERVES FOR
8 PEOPLE

INGREDIENTS

1/4 teaspoon salt
1/2 teaspoon crushed red pepper
1 clove garlic, thinly sliced
1 tablespoon minced flat-leaf parsley, plus a few sprigs for garnish
1 tablespoon extra-virgin olive oil
1 tablespoon butter
2 bay leaves, preferably fresh
2 teaspoons lemon juice, plus lemon wedges for garnish
3/4 cup dry white wine
3/4 cup low-sodium chicken broth
24 unpeeled raw shrimp, preferably with heads left on

NUTRITION FACTS

Per Serving:

136 calories
protein 20.4g
carbohydrates 1g
fat 3.9g
cholesterol 162.6mg
sodium 185 mg

STEPS

1. Rinse shrimp and pat dry. Gently separate bodies from heads. Peel all but the tail (keeping the heads and shells); set aside.
2. Combine broth, wine, bay leaves, shrimp shells, and heads in a skillet. Bring to a boil over medium-high heat. Reduce heat to maintain a simmer, cover, and cook for 6 minutes. Uncover and cook at a lively simmer for 5 minutes more. Strain the stock into a bowl and discard the solids. Wipe out the pan.
3. Heat butter and oil in the pan over medium-low heat. Add garlic and cook, stirring, until softened but not browned, for about 2 minutes. Add crushed red pepper, salt, and shrimp stock. Increase heat to medium-high and cook until reduced by half, about 4 minutes.
4. Arrange the reserved shrimp in the pan in a single layer, cook for 2 minutes per side. Add lemon juice and parsley and toss gently to combine. Transfer the shrimp to a warm platter. Serve with lemon wedges and more parsley.

Sauteed Shrimp and Asparagus

INGREDIENTS

1/4 cup dry red wine or reduced-sodium chicken broth
1/4 cup finely chopped green onions
1 teaspoon toasted sesame oil
1 pound fresh large shrimp in shells
2 teaspoons canola oil
2 teaspoons minced fresh garlic
2 teaspoons grated fresh ginger root
8 ounces fresh asparagus spears, trimmd
Lemon Herbed Orzo Pasta

STEPS

1. Peel shrimp. Rinse shrimp; pat dry with paper towels.
2. In a nonstick skillet, cook shrimp in hot canola and sesame oil over medium heat for 3 minutes. Add garlic and ginger; cook 3 minutes more, turning occasionally. Remove shrimp from skillet; set aside.
3. Carefully add wine and asparagus to the hot skillet. Cover and cook for 4 minutes. Add shrimp and green onions to skillet, and stir until warm. Serve!

NUTRITION FACTS

Per Serving:

304 calories
protein 24.1g
carbohydrates 36g
fat 5.6g
cholesterol 129.3mg
sodium 257mg

Baked Cod with Lemon and Garlic

PREPARATION
10 MIN

SERVES FOR
5 PEOPLE

INGREDIENTS

1/4 cup chopped fresh parsley leaves
1.5 lb Cod fillet pieces
5 garlic cloves, peeled and minced
   Lemon Juice Mixture
2 tbsp melted butter
5 tbsp fresh lemon juice
5 tbsp extra virgin olive oil
   For Coating
1/3 cup all-purpose flour
1/2 tsp black pepper
1 tsp ground coriander
3/4 tsp sweet paprika
3/4 tsp ground cumin
3/4 tsp salt

NUTRITION FACTS

Per Serving:

311 calories
protein 25.5g
carbohydrates 8g
fat 19.8g
cholesterol 70.6mg
sodium 466.1mg

STEPS

1. Preheat oven to 425 degrees F.
2. Mix olive oil, lemon juice, and melted butter in a shallow bowl. Set aside
3. In another shallow bowl, mix all-purpose flour, spices, salt, and pepper. Set next to the lemon juice mixture.
4. Pat fish fillet dry. Dip fish in the lemon juice mixture then dip in the flour mixture. Shake off excess flour. Reserve the lemon juice mixture for later.
5. Heat 2 tbsp olive oil in a cast-iron skillet over medium heat. Add fish and sear on each side to give it some color, but do not fully cook. Remove from heat.
6. To the remaining lemon juice mixture, add the minced garlic and mix. Combine all over the fish fillets.
7. Bake in the heated for about 9 minutes. Remove from heat and garnish with chopped parsley. Serve immediately.

Smoked Salmon Platter

PREPARATION
15 MIN

SERVES FOR
6 PEOPLE

INGREDIENTS

1/4 cup assorted olives
1/3 cup marinated artichoke hearts
1 bell pepper hinly sliced into rounds
1 English cucumber, thinly sliced into rounds
1 vine-ripe tomato, thinly sliced into rounds
1 small red onion, thinly sliced into rounds
1 lemon, cut into wedges
3 oz Feta cheese, sliced into slabs
4 oz Cream cheese
4 eggs, soft boiled
5 radishes, thinly sliced into rounds
12 oz smoked salmon
Salt
Red pepper flakes

NUTRITION FACTS

Per Serving:

198 calories
protein 20.3g
carbohydrates 9.6g
fat 2.1g
cholesterol 130.7mg

STEPS

1. Bring a saucepan of water to a boil over medium heat, and boil the eggs. Cook for exactly 7 1/2 minutes, adjusting the heat as necessary to maintain a gentle boil. When the eggs are ready, transfer them to a large bowl of iced water and let them sit for about 3 minutes. Peel the eggs and cut them in halves and season with salt and a pinch of red pepper flakes.

2. To assemble the salmon platter, place a bowl of cream cheese in one-third of the platter. Place the feta cheese in another corner of the platter. Arrange the salmon, bell peppers, radish, cucumbers, olives, tomatoes, onions, artichoke hearts, and lemon wedges around the cheese. Season with a little pepper.

3. Serve!

Fish en Papillote

PREPARATION
10 MIN

SERVES FOR
4 PEOPLE

INGREDIENTS

1/2 tomato thinly sliced into 4 rounds
1/2 green bell pepper cored, thinly sliced into 4 rounds
1/2 lemon thinly sliced into rings
1 1/4 lb cod fish fillet (1-inch thick) cut into 4 pieces
Salt and black pepper
Handful pitted green olives
For the Sauce
1/4 cup extra virgin olive oil
1/2 tsp cumin
1 shallot chopped
1 tsp oregano
1 tsp paprika
2 garlic cloves chopped
Juice of 1/2 lemon

NUTRITION FACTS

Per Serving:

221 calories
protein 26.1g
carbohydrates 4.9g
fat 11.7g
sodium 370mg

STEPS

1. Prepare the sauce. Place the olive oil, lemon juice, garlic, shallots, and spices in a mixing bowl and whisk to combine.
2. Heat the oven to 425 degrees F.
3. Season the fish with salt and pepper on both sides.
4. Prepare 4 large pieces of parchment paper. Fold the parchment paper pieces down the middle to mark two halves.
5. Assemble the pouches. Place each fish fillet on the bottom half of a parchment piece. Spoon 2 tablespoons of the prepared sauce over the fish. Add 1 lemon slice, 1 bell pepper slice, and 1 tomato slice, on top.
6. Fold the top half of the parchment paper over the fish and veggies and go around to fold and secure each piece of parchment around the fish and veggies creating a well-wrapped pouch.
7. Place the fish pouches on a baking sheet. Bake on the middle rack of your heated oven for 15 minutes.
8. To serve, leave the fish and veggies in their own closed parchment pouches and transfer each pouch to a serving plate. Serve!

Fajita-Style Shrimp and Grits

PREPARATION
15 MIN

SERVES FOR
4 PEOPLE

INGREDIENTS

1/4 cup orange juice
1/4 cup plus 1 tablespoon fresh cilantro leaves, divided
1 cup quick-cooking grits
1 medium sweet onion, cut
1 pound uncooked shrimp, peeled and deveined
1 jar (15-1/2 to 16 ounces) chunky medium salsa
1-1/2 cups shredded Mexican cheese blend
2 tablespoons canola oil
2 tablespoons fajita seasoning mix
3 medium sweet peppers, seeded and cut
3 tablespoons 2% milk
4 cups boiling water

STEPS

1. Sprinkle shrimp with fajita seasoning; mix to coat. Set aside.
2. Slowly stir grits into boiling water. Reduce heat to medium; cook, covered, stirring occasionally, for about 6 minutes. Remove from heat. Stir in cheese until melted; stir in milk. Keep warm.
3. In a skillet, heat oil over medium heat. Add onion and peppers; cook and stir. Add salsa, shrimp, and orange juice. Cook, stirring constantly, for about 5 minutes. Stir in 1/4 cup cilantro. Remove from heat.
4. Garnish with shrimp mixture. Sprinkle with remaining cilantro. Serve!

NUTRITION FACTS

Per Serving:

561 calories
protein 33g
carbohydrates 55g
fat 23g
cholesterol 176mg

Sheet-Pan Chipotle-Lime Shrimp Bake

PREPARATION
10 MIN

SERVES FOR
4 PEOPLE

INGREDIENTS

1/4 cup unsalted butter, melted
1/2 pound Broccolini, cut into small florets
1/2 pound fresh asparagus, trimmed
1 tablespoon extra virgin olive oil
1 teaspoon ground chipotle pepper
1 pound uncooked shrimp (16-20 per pound), peeled and deveined
1-1/2 pounds baby red potatoes, cut into 3/4-inch cubes
2 tablespoons minced fresh cilantro
3 medium limes
3/4 teaspoon sea salt, divided

STEPS

1. Preheat oven to 400F. Place potatoes in a greased baking pan; drizzle with olive oil. Sprinkle with 1/4 teaspoon sea salt; stir to combine. Bake 35 minutes. Meanwhile, squeeze 1/3 cup juice from limes, reserving fruit. Combine lime juice, melted butter, chipotle, and remaining sea salt.
2. Remove sheet pan from oven; stir potatoes. Arrange asparagus, shrimp, Broccolini, and reserved limes on top of potatoes. Pour lime juice mixture over vegetables and shrimp.
3. Bake for about 12 minutes longer. Garnish with cilantro. Serve!

NUTRITION FACTS

Per Serving:

394 calories
protein 25g
carbohydrates 41g
fat 17g
cholesterol 168mg
sodium 535mg

Shrimp with Curry

PREPARATION
30 MIN

SERVES FOR
6 PEOPLE

INGREDIENTS

1/4 teaspoon ground mustard
1/2 cup heavy whipping cream
1/2 teaspoon salt
1 large onion, chopped
1 medium tart apple, peeled and finely chopped
1 celery rib, chopped
1 garlic clove, minced
1 bay leaf
1-1/2 pounds uncooked medium shrimp, peeled and deveined
2 tablespoons butter
2 tablespoons all-purpose flour
2 cups chicken stock
2 teaspoons curry powder
Hot cooked rice

STEPS

1. In a saucepan, heat butter over medium heat. Add onion, celery, and apple; cook and stir until tender, for 4 minutes. Add garlic; cook 1 minute longer. Stir in flour until blended; gradually whisk in chicken stock, cream, mustard, curry powder, salt, and bay leaf. Bring to a boil, stirring constantly; cook and stir until thickened, for 4 minutes.
2. Reduce heat; simmer, uncovered, for about 8 minutes, stirring occasionally. Add shrimp; cook, for 7 minutes. Serve with rice.

NUTRITION FACTS

Per Serving:

239 calories
protein 21g
carbohydrates 10g
fat 13g
cholesterol 171mg
sodium 544mg

Shrimp Chowder

PREPARATION
30 MIN

SERVES FOR
4 PEOPLE

INGREDIENTS

1/4 cup butter, cubed
1/4 cup all-purpose flour
1/2 pound cooked small shrimp, peeled and deveined
1/2 cup each chopped onion, celery, carrot and sweet red pepper
1 teaspoon minced fresh thyme
1 cup vegetable broth
1 cup frozen corn, thawed
2 cups 2% milk
2 teaspoons seafood seasoning
14-1/2 ounces diced potatoes, drained

STEPS

1. In a saucepan, saute the onion, carrot, celery, and red pepper in butter for 6 minutes. Stir in flour until blended; gradually add milk. Bring to a boil; cook and stir for 3 minutes.
2. Add the potatoes, shrimp, broth, corn, seafood seasoning, and thyme. Reduce heat; cover and simmer for 12 minutes. Garnish with additional minced fresh thyme. Serve!

NUTRITION FACTS

Per Serving:

268 calories
protein 16g
carbohydrates 25g
fat 12g
cholesterol 120mg
sodium 901mg

Spicy Shrimp & Penne Pasta

PREPARATION
30 MIN

SERVES FOR
6 PEOPLE

INGREDIENTS

1/2 teaspoon crushed red pepper flakes
1 tablespoon olive oil
1 tablespoon butter
2 pounds uncooked shrimp, peeled and deveined
3 cups uncooked penne pasta
3/4 cup half-and-half cream
4 cups chopped fresh spinach
24 ounces marinara sauce

STEPS

1. Cook pasta according to package directions; drain.
2. In a skillet, heat 1/2 tablespoon each butter and oil over medium heat. Saute 1 pound shrimp with 1/4 teaspoon pepper flakes for 6 minutes. Remove from pan; repeat.
3. In the same skillet, combine marinara sauce and cream; bring to a boil over medium heat. Stir in spinach until wilted. Add pasta and shrimp; toss and heat through. Serve!

NUTRITION FACTS

Per Serving:

396 calories
protein 33g
carbohydrates 38g
fat 12g
cholesterol 206mg
sodium 723mg

Grilled Pistachio-Lemon Pesto Shrimp

PREPARATION
20 MIN

SERVES FOR
8 PEOPLE

INGREDIENTS

3/4 cup fresh arugula
1/2 cup minced fresh parsley
1/3 cup shelled pistachios
2 tablespoons lemon juice
1 garlic clove, peeled
1/4 teaspoon grated lemon zest
1/2 cup olive oil
1/4 cup shredded Parmesan cheese
1/4 teaspoon salt
1/8 teaspoon pepper
1-1/2 pounds uncooked jumbo shrimp, peeled and deveined

STEPS

1. Place the first 6 ingredients in a food processor; pulse until finely chopped. Continue processing while gradually adding oil in a steady stream. Add Parmesan cheese, salt, and pepper; pulse just until combined. Transfer 1/3 cup pesto to a bowl. Add shrimp; toss to coat. Refrigerate, covered, 40 minutes.

2. Thread shrimp onto 8 soaked wooden skewers; place on greased grill rack. Cook, covered, over medium heat until shrimp turn pink, for 6 minutes, turning once. Serve with remaining pesto.

NUTRITION FACTS

Per Serving:

236 calories
protein 16g
carbohydrates 13g
fat 18g
cholesterol 105mg
sodium 241mg

Shrimp Pad Thai

PREPARATION
25 MIN

SERVES FOR
4 PEOPLE

INGREDIENTS

1/4 cup sugar
1/3 cup rice vinegar
1 large onion, chopped
1 garlic clove, minced
1 large egg, lightly beaten
1/2 pound uncooked small shrimp, peeled and deveined
2 tablespoons chopped salted peanuts
2 teaspoons canola oil
2 tablespoons fish sauce
3 teaspoons chili garlic sauce
3 cups coleslaw mix
3 tablespoons reduced-sodium soy sauce
4 ounces uncooked thick rice noodles
4 green onions, thinly sliced
Chopped fresh cilantro leaves

STEPS

1. Cook noodles according to package directions.
2. In a large nonstick, stir-fry shrimp in oil until shrimp turn pink; remove and set aside. Add garlic, and onion to the pan. Make a well in the center of the onion mixture; add the egg. Stir-fry for 3 minutes.
3. Add the coleslaw mix, vinegar, green onions, sugar, fish sauce, soy sauce, chili garlic sauce, and peanuts; heat through. Return shrimp to the pan and heat through. Drain noodles; toss with shrimp mixture. Garnish with cilantro. Serve!

NUTRITION FACTS

Per Serving:

338calories
protein 17g
carbohydrates 52g
fat 7g
cholesterol 115mg

Coconut Shrimp Chowder

PREPARATION
30 MIN

SERVES FOR
5 PEOPLE

INGREDIENTS

1/4 teaspoon pepper
1/4 cup lime juice
1/4 teaspoon salt
1/4 teaspoon pepper
1 medium ripe avocado, peeled and cubed
1 medium onion, chopped
1 pound uncooked medium shrimp, peeled and deveined
2 teaspoons canola oil
2 tablespoons minced fresh cilantro
2 cups chicken broth
10 ounces frozen corn
13.66 ounces coconut milk

STEPS

1. In a saucepan, saute onion in oil until tender, add pepper. Stir in the broth, corn, salt, and pepper. Bring to a boil. Reduce heat; simmer, uncovered, for 6 minutes. Remove from the heat and stir in coconut milk. Cool slightly.
2. In a food processor, process soup in batches until blended. Return all to the pan. Add shrimp; cook and stir over medium heat for 7 minutes. Stir in lime juice and cilantro. Garnish servings with avocado. Serve!

NUTRITION FACTS

Per Serving:

calories 376kcal
carbohydrates 22g
protein 20g
fat 26g
cholesterol 112mg
sodium 633mg

Shrimp Soup

PREPARATION
25 MIN

SERVES FOR
6 PEOPLE

INGREDIENTS

1/4 teaspoon salt
1/4 teaspoon pepper
1 medium sweet red pepper, cut into 3/4-inch pieces
1 bunch kale, trimmed and coarsely chopped
1 pound uncooked shrimp, peeled and deveined
3 cups reduced-sodium chicken broth
4 teaspoons olive oil, divided
5 garlic cloves, minced
15-1/2 ounces black-eyed peas, rinsed and drained
Minced fresh chives

STEPS

1. In a stockpot, heat 2 teaspoons oil over medium heat. Add shrimp; cook and stir for 3 minutes. Add garlic; cook just until shrimp turn pink, for 1 minute longer. Remove from pot.
2. In the same pot, heat the remaining oil over medium heat. Stir in kale and red pepper; cook, covered, stirring occasionally, for 12 minutes. Add broth; bring to a boil. Stir in peas, salt, pepper, and shrimp. Sprinkle servings with chives. Serve!

NUTRITION FACTS

Per Serving:

calories 188kcal
carbohydrates 18g
protein 19g
fat 5g
cholesterol 92mg
sodium 585mg

PREPARATION
15 MIN

SERVES FOR
4 PEOPLE

Mediterranean Shrimp Pasta

NUTRITION FACTS

Per Serving:
368 calories; fat 6g; carbohydrates 46g; protein 32g; cholesterol 173mg; sodium 702mg

INGREDIENTS

1/4 teaspoon pepper
1/2 cup thinly sliced green onions
1/2 cup dry-pack sun-dried tomatoes, chopped
1 pound uncooked medium shrimp, peeled and deveined
1 teaspoon curry powder
1 pound fresh asparagus, trimmed and cut into 1-inch pieces
1 tablespoon olive oil
1 cup boiling water
2 tablespoons clam juice
2 tablespoons unsweetened apple juice
2 garlic cloves, minced
6 ounces uncooked fettuccine
8 ounces tomato sauce

STEPS

1. In a bowl, pour boiling water over sun-dried tomatoes; let stand for 3 minutes. Drain and set aside. Cook fettuccine according to package directions.
2. Meanwhile, in a bowl, combine juice clam, the tomato sauce, apple juice, curry powder, and pepper; set aside. In a nonstick skillet coated with cooking spray, cook asparagus in oil for 3 minutes. Add green onions and garlic; cook and stir 1 minute longer.
3. Stir in shrimp. Cook and stir 4 minutes longer. Stir in tomato sauce mixture and sun-dried tomatoes; heat through. Drain fettuccine and add to skillet; toss to coat.
4. Serve!

Spicy Shrimp with Rice

PREPARATION
15 MIN

SERVES FOR
8 PEOPLE

INGREDIENTS

1/4 teaspoon onion salt
1/4 teaspoon pepper
1/2 cup minced fresh parsley
1/2 cup reduced-sodium chicken broth
1 large onion, finely chopped
1 large green pepper, chopped
1 tablespoon olive oil
2 tablespoons Louisiana-style hot sauce
2 pounds uncooked large shrimp, peeled and deveined
3 garlic cloves, minced
4 ounces diced pimientos, drained
5-2/3 cups hot cooked rice
8 ounces tomato sauce

STEPS

1. In a skillet, saute the onion and green pepper in oil until tender. Add garlic; cook 1 minute longer. Stir in broth, tomato sauce, pimientos, parsley, hot sauce, onion salt, and pepper.
2. Bring to a boil. Reduce heat; cover and simmer for 12 minutes, stirring occasionally. Stir in shrimp; cook for 7 minutes longer. Serve with rice.

NUTRITION FACTS

Per Serving:

Calories: 273kcal
Carbohydrates: 37g
Protein: 22g
Fat:3g
Cholesterol: 168mg
Sodium: 425mg

Scrumptious California Salmon

PREPARATION
35 MIN

SERVES FOR
4 PEOPLE

INGREDIENTS

1/8 teaspoon pepper
1/4 teaspoon salt
1 tablespoon balsamic vinegar
1 teaspoon minced shallot
1 cup orange juice
1 salmon fillet
1 tablespoon ground ancho chili pepper
2 teaspoons canola oil
2 tablespoons minced fresh cilantro
3 garlic cloves, minced
3 tablespoons honey

STEPS

1. In a saucepan coated with cooking spray, saute shallot, and garlic for 2 minutes. Add vinegar, and orange juice. Bring to a boil. Reduce heat; simmer, uncovered until reduced to 1/4 cup, for 25 minutes. Stir in the honey, chili pepper, salt, and pepper.
2. In a cast-iron or other ovenproof skillet, brown salmon in oil, about 4 minutes on each side. Brush with sauce. Bake, uncovered, at 425 F, for about 9 minutes.
3. Brush with any remaining sauce and sprinkle with cilantro. Serve!

NUTRITION FACTS

Per Serving:

Calories: 317kcal
Carbohydrates: 21g
Protein: 23g
Fat: 15g
Cholesterol: 67mg
Sodium: 217mg

Greek Salmon Salad

PREPARATION
5 MIN

SERVES FOR
4 PEOPLE

INGREDIENTS

For Salmon
1 lb salmon fillet cut into 4 equal pieces
Salt and black pepper
Dried oregano a generous pinch 1 1/2 tsp or more to your liking

For the Lemon-Mint Vinaigrette
1/2 tsp sweet paprika
1/2 cup quality extra virgin olive oil
1 tsp dried oregano
2 large lemons
2 garlic cloves roughly chopped
20 to 30 fresh mint leaves no stems

For Salad
1 bell pepper any color, cored and sliced into rounds
1 English cucumber sliced into rounds
2 shallots sliced
8 oz chopped hearts of Romaine lettuce
10 oz cherry or grape tomatoes
Pitted olives
Greek feta blocks

NUTRITION FACTS

Per Serving:

Calories: 474kcal
Carbohydrates: 17.8g
Protein: 25.8g
Fat: 5g
Cholesterol: 62mg
Sodium: 356mg

STEPS

1. Preheat the oven to 400 degrees F and position a rack in the middle.
2. Season the salmon. Pat the salmon dry on both sides and season with salt, pepper, and dried oregano. Arrange on a lightly oiled sheet pan and brush the top of the salmon with extra virgin olive oil.
3. Bake the salmon in the heated oven for 14 minutes. Meanwhile, work on the salad and the vinaigrette.
4. Prepare the salad. In a large salad bowl, add the lettuce, cucumbers, tomatoes, shallots, bell peppers, and olives (don't add the feta yet).
5. Prepare the vinaigrette. In the bowl of a food processor fitted with a blade, add olive oil, garlic, oregano, lemon juice, fresh mint, and paprika. Add a pinch of salt and black pepper. Blend until well-combined.
6. Pour about 1/2 of the vinaigrette over the salad. Mix to combine. Now add the feta cheese blocks on top. Hold the remaining vinaigrette to dress the salmon later.
7. Build your salmon salad bowls. Transfer the salad to 4 serving bowls, top each with 1 fillet of salmon. Add the remaining vinaigrette on top of the salmon. Serve!

Maple-Glazed Salmon

PREPARATION
10 MIN

SERVES FOR
4 PEOPLE

INGREDIENTS

1/4 cup ruby red grapefruit juice
1/4 teaspoon salt
1/4 teaspoon pepper
2 tablespoons balsamic vinegar
2 tablespoons maple syrup
2 garlic cloves, minced
2 teaspoons olive oil
4 salmon fillets
Fresh thyme sprigs

STEPS

1. In a saucepan, bring vinegar, grapefruit juice, syrup, and garlic to a boil. Reduce heat; simmer, uncovered, for 6 minutes. Transfer 2 tablespoons to a small bowl; add oil. Set remaining glaze aside.

2. Sprinkle salmon with salt and pepper; place skin side down on grill rack. Using long-handled tongs, moisten a paper towel with cooking oil and lightly coat the grill rack. Broil heat until fish flakes easily with a fork, for about 12 minutes, basting occasionally the maple-oil mixture. Drizzle with reserved 2 Tbsp. Garnish with fresh thyme sprigs. Serve!

NUTRITION FACTS

Per Serving:

Calories: 266kcal
Carbohydrates: 10g
Protein: 23g
Fat: 15g
Cholesterol: 67mg
Sodium: 218mg

Sesame Salmon with Wasabi Mayo

PREPARATION
15 MIN

SERVES FOR
6 PEOPLE

INGREDIENTS

1/4 teaspoon salt
1/4 teaspoon pepper
1/3 cup mayonnaise
1 salmon fillet
1 teaspoon prepared wasabi
1-1/2 teaspoons lemon juice
2 tablespoons sesame seeds, toasted
2 tablespoons butter, melted
3 tablespoons sesame oil, divided
4 green onions, chopped

STEPS

1. Drizzle butter and 2 tablespoons oil into a baking dish; tilt to coat bottom. Place salmon in the dish; brush with remaining oil and sprinkle with salt and pepper.
2. Bake, uncovered, at 425 F, for 22 minutes. Meanwhile, combine the mayonnaise, lemon juice and wasabi. Sprinkle salmon with onions and sesame seeds. Serve with sauce.

NUTRITION FACTS

Per Serving:

Calories: 439kcal
Carbohydrates: 2g
Protein: 26g
Fat: 36g
Fiber: 1g
Cholesterol: 90mg
Sodium: 302mg

Seared Salmon with Basil Sauce

PREPARATION
10 MIN

SERVES FOR
5 PEOPLE

INGREDIENTS

1/8 teaspoon freshly ground pepper
1/4 teaspoon salt
1 tablespoon butter, melted
1 tablespoon honey
1 tablespoon minced fresh basil
1-1/4 cups finely chopped fresh strawberries
6 salmon fillets (4 ounces each)
Dash freshly ground pepper

STEPS

1. Brush fillets with melted butter; sprinkle with salt and pepper. Heat a skillet over medium heat. Add fillets, skin side up, in batches if necessary; cook for 6 minutes totals.
2. In a bowl, toss strawberries with honey, basil, and pepper, and serve.

NUTRITION FACTS

Per Serving:

Calories: 215kcal
Carbohydrates: 6g
Protein: 19g
Fat: 12g
Saturated Fat: 3g
Fiber: 1g
Cholesterol: 62mg
Sodium: 169mg

Salmon with Spinach & White Beans

PREPARATION
5 MIN

SERVES FOR
5 PEOPLE

INGREDIENTS

1/4 teaspoon salt
1/4 teaspoon pepper
1 teaspoon seafood seasoning
1 garlic clove, minced
2 teaspoons plus 1 tablespoon olive oil, divided
4 salmon fillets (4 ounces each)
15 ounces cannellini beans, rinsed and drained
8 ounces fresh spinach
Lemon wedges

STEPS

1. Preheat broiler. Rub fillets with 2 teaspoons oil; sprinkle with seafood seasoning. Place on a greased broiler pan. Grill for 8 minutes or until fish just begins to flake easily with a fork.
2. Meanwhile, in a skillet, heat the remaining oil over medium heat. Add garlic; cook for 40 seconds. Add beans, salt, and pepper, stirring to coat beans with garlic oil. Stir in spinach until wilted. Serve salmon with spinach mixture and lemon wedges.

NUTRITION FACTS

Per Serving:

Calories: 317kcal
Carbohydrates: 16g
Protein: 24g
Fat: 17g
SaturatedFat: 3g
Fiber: 5g
Cholesterol: 57mg
Sodium: 577mg

Salmon with Garlic and Lime

PREPARATION
10 MIN

SERVES FOR
8 PEOPLE

INGREDIENTS

1/2 cup canola oil
1 garlic clove, minced
1 medium onion, finely chopped
1 teaspoon grated lime zest
2 tablespoons lime juice
2 salmon fillets (about 1-1/2 pounds each)

STEPS

1. Preheat broiler. In a bowl, mix the canola oil, garlic, onion, lime zest, and lime juice.
2. Place salmon fillets on a broiler pan, skin side down. Broil until fish just begins to flake easily with a fork, about 20 minutes. Brush frequently with onion mixture during the last 5 minutes of cooking.
3. Serve!

NUTRITION FACTS

Per Serving:

Calories: 380kcal
Carbohydrates: 3g
Protein: 23g
Fat: 30g
Saturated Fat: 5g
Fiber: 1g
Cholesterol: 67mg
Sodium: 68mg

Spicy Salmon Patties

PREPARATION
15 MIN

SERVES FOR
4 PEOPLE

INGREDIENTS

2 slices whole wheat bread
12 miniature pretzels
2 teaspoons Italian seasoning
2 teaspoons salt-free spicy seasoning blend
1/2 teaspoon pepper
2 large eggs, lightly beaten
1 can (14-3/4 ounces) salmon, drained, bones and skin removed
1/2 cup finely chopped onion
1/3 cup finely chopped green pepper
1 tablespoon finely chopped jalapeno pepper
2 garlic cloves, minced
2 tablespoons olive oil

STEPS

1. Place the first 5 ingredients in a blender; cover and process until mixture resemble fine crumbs.
2. In a bowl, combine onion, eggs, salmon, jalapeno, green pepper, garlic, and 1/2 cup crumb mixture. Shape into eight 1/2-in.-thick patties. Coat with the remaining crumb mixture.
3. In a nonstick skillet over medium heat, cook patties in oil until golden brown, for 5 minutes on each side. Serve!

NUTRITION FACTS

Per Serving:

Calories: 339kcal
Carbohydrates: 13g
Protein: 30g
Fat: 18g
Saturated Fat: 3g
Fiber: 2g
Cholesterol: 176mg
Sodium: 607mg

Orange Pomegranate Salmon

INGREDIENTS

1/2 teaspoon salt
1 small red onion, thinly sliced
1 skinned salmon fillet (about 2 pounds)
1 tablespoon minced fresh dill
1 medium navel orange, thinly sliced
1 cup pomegranate seeds
2 tablespoons extra virgin olive oil

STEPS

1. Preheat oven to 400 F. Places piece of foil in a baking pan. Place onion slices in a single layer on foil. Add salmon; sprinkle with salt. Arrange orange slices over top. Sprinkle with pomegranate seeds; drizzle with oil. Top with the second piece of foil. Bring edges of foil together on all sides and crimp to seal, forming a large packet.
2. Bake, for 25 minutes. Remove to a serving platter; Garnish with dill. Serve!

NUTRITION FACTS

Per Serving:

Calories: 307kcal
Carbohydrates: 8g
Protein: 26g
Fat: 19g
Fiber: 1g
Cholesterol: 76mg
Sodium: 274mg

Salmon with Roasted Tomatoes & Artichokes

PREPARATION
15 MIN

SERVES FOR
4 PEOPLE

INGREDIENTS

1/4 teaspoon pepper, divided
1 medium sweet yellow pepper, cut into 1-inch pieces
2 cups grape tomatoes
4 salmon fillets
5 tablespoons reduced-fat Caesar vinaigrette, divided
14 ounces water-packed artichoke hearts, drained and quartered

STEPS

1. Preheat oven to 400 F. Place salmon on half of a baking pan coated with cooking spray. Brush with 2 tablespoons vinaigrette; sprinkle with 1/8 teaspoon pepper.
2. In a bowl, combine artichoke hearts, tomatoes, and sweet pepper. Add the remaining vinaigrette and pepper. Place tomato mixture on the remaining half of the pan. Roast the fish and vegetables, for 17 minutes. Serve!

NUTRITION FACTS

Per Serving:

Calories: 318kcal
Carbohydrates: 12g
Protein: 28g
Fat: 16g
Saturated Fat: 3g
Fiber: 2g
Cholesterol: 73mg
Sodium: 674mg

Salmon with Brown Sugar Glaze

PREPARATION
15 MIN

SERVES FOR
8 PEOPLE

INGREDIENTS

1/4 teaspoon pepper
1 tablespoon brown sugar
1 teaspoon honey
1 tablespoon olive oil
1 tablespoon mustard
1 tablespoon reduced-sodium soy sauce
1 salmon fillet (2-1/2 pounds)
2 teaspoons butter
3/4 teaspoon salt

STEPS

1. In a saucepan over medium heat, cook and stir the brown sugar, butter, and honey until melted. Remove from the heat; whisk in the oil, soy sauce, mustard, salt, and pepper. Cool for 6 minutes.
2. Place salmon in a foil-lined baking pan; spoon brown sugar mixture over top. Bake at 375 F for 22 minutes. Serve!

NUTRITION FACTS

Per Serving:

Calories: 295kcal
Carbohydrates: 3g
Protein: 28g
Fat: 18g
Saturated Fat: 3g
Fiber: 0g
Cholesterol: 84mg
Sodium: 403 mg

Creamy Scallop & Pea Fettuccine

PREPARATION
40 MIN

SERVES FOR
4 PEOPLE

INGREDIENTS

1/4 teaspoon ground white pepper
1/4 teaspoon salt, divided
1/3 cup chopped fresh chives
1/2 teaspoon freshly grated lemon zest
1 pound large dry sea scallops,
1 tablespoon extra-virgin olive oil
1 teaspoon lemon juice
1 cup low-fat milk
1 8-ounce bottle clam juice,
3 tablespoons all-purpose flour
3 cups frozen peas, thawed
3/4 cup finely shredded Romano cheese, divided
8 ounces whole-wheat fettuccine

STEPS

1. Bring a pot of water to a boil. Cook fettuccine until just tender, for about 10 minutes. Drain.
2. Meanwhile, pat scallops dry and sprinkle with 1/8 teaspoon salt. Heat oil in a nonstick skillet over medium heat. Add the scallops and cook until golden brown, for 6 minutes totals. Transfer to a plate.
3. Add clam juice to the pan. Whisk milk, flour, white pepper, and the remaining 1/8 teaspoon salt in a bowl until smooth. Whisk the milk mixture into the clam juice. Bring the mixture to a simmer, stirring constantly. Continue stirring until thickened, 1 to 2 minutes. Return the scallops and any accumulated juices to the pan along with peas and return to a simmer. Stir in the fettuccine, 1/2 cup Romano cheese, chives, lemon zest, and lemon juice until combined. Garnish with the remaining cheese sprinkled on top.

NUTRITION FACTS

Per Serving:

Calories: 413kcal
Carbohydrates: 55g
Protein: 29.5g
Fat: 9.4g
Cholesterol: 38.6mg
Sodium: 938mg

Speedy Salmon Patties

PREPARATION
5 MIN

SERVES FOR
3 PEOPLE

INGREDIENTS

1/8 teaspoon pepper
1/4 teaspoon salt
1/3 cup finely chopped onion
1/2 teaspoon Worcestershire sauce
1 large egg, beaten
2 teaspoons butter
5 saltines, crushed
14-3/4 ounces salmon, drained, bones and skin removed

STEPS

1. In a bowl, combine onion, Worcestershire sauce, egg, saltines, salt, and pepper. Crumble salmon over mixture and mix well. Shape into 6 patties.
2. In a skillet over medium heat, fry patties in butter for 4 minutes on each side.
3. Serve!

NUTRITION FACTS

Per Serving:

Calories: 288kcal
Carbohydrates: 5g
Protein: 31g
Fat: 15g
Saturated Fat: 4g
Fiber: 0g
Cholesterol: 139mg

Sweet-Chili Salmon with Blackberries

PREPARATION
10 MIN

SERVES FOR
4 PEOPLE

INGREDIENTS

1/2 teaspoon salt
1/2 teaspoon pepper
1 cup fresh blackberries, thawed
1 cup finely chopped English cucumber
1 green onion, finely chopped
2 tablespoons sweet chili sauce, divided
4 salmon fillets (6 ounces each)

STEPS

1. In a bowl, combine cucumber, blackberries, green onion, and 1 tablespoon chili sauce; and mix. Sprinkle salmon with salt and pepper.

2. Place fillets on greased grill rack, skin side down. Grill, covered, over medium heat for 13 minutes, brushing with remaining chili sauce during the last 3 minutes of cooking. Serve with a blackberry mixture.

NUTRITION FACTS

Per Serving:

Calories: 303kcal
Carbohydrates: 9g
Protein: 30g
Fat: 16g
Saturated Fat: 3g
Cholesterol: 85mg
Sodium: 510mg

Salmon Veggie Packets

PREPARATION
10 MIN

SERVES FOR
4 PEOPLE

INGREDIENTS

1/4 teaspoon salt
1/4 teaspoon pepper
1 tablespoon olive oil
2 tablespoons white wine
2 medium sweet yellow peppers, julienned
2 cups fresh sugar snap peas, trimmed
Salmon
1/4 teaspoon pepper
1/2 teaspoon salt
1 medium lemon, halved
1 tablespoon grated lemon zest
1 tablespoon olive oil
2 tablespoons white wine
4 salmon fillets

NUTRITION FACTS

Per Serving:

Calories: 400kcal
Carbohydrates: 13g
Protein: 32g
Fat: 23g
SaturatedFat: 4g
Fiber: 3g
Cholesterol: 85mg
Sodium: 535mg

STEPS

1. Preheat oven to 425 F. Cut 4 pieces of parchment paper foil: fold each crosswise in half, forming a crease. In a bowl, mix wine, oil, salt, and pepper. Add vegetables and toss to coat.
2. In a small bowl, mix the first five salmon ingredients. To assemble, lay open one piece of parchment paper; place a salmon fillet on one side. Drizzle with 2 teaspoons wine mixture; add one-fourth of the vegetables.
3. Fold the paper over fish and vegetables; fold the open ends two times to seal. Repeat with the remaining packets. Place on baking sheets.
4. Bake until fish just begins to flake easily with a fork, for 15 minutes.
5. Garnish with lemon juice. Serve!

Asian Salmon Tacos

PREPARATION
5 MIN

SERVES FOR
4 PEOPLE

INGREDIENTS

1 pound salmon fillet, skin removed, cut into
1-inch cubes
1-1/2 teaspoons black sesame seeds
1 tablespoon olive oil
2 tablespoons hoisin sauce
8 corn tortillas, warmed
Mango salsa
Shredded lettuce

STEPS

1. Season salmon with hoisin sauce. In a nonstick skillet, heat oil over medium heat. Cook salmon until it begins to flake easily with a fork, for about 6 minutes, turning gently to brown all sides.
2. Serve salmon and lettuce in tortillas; sprinkle with sesame seeds, top with salsa. Serve!

NUTRITION FACTS

Per Serving:

Calories: 335kcal
Carbohydrates: 25g
Protein: 22g
Fat: 16g
Cholesterol: 57mg

Salmon & Spinach Salad

PREPARATION
10 MIN

SERVES FOR
2 PEOPLE

INGREDIENTS

1/8 teaspoon pepper
1/4 cup crumbled feta cheese
1/2 teaspoon Greek seasoning
1/2 cup quinoa, rinsed
1 cup reduced-sodium chicken broth
1 teaspoon olive oil
1 cup grape tomatoes, halved
1 tablespoon minced fresh oregano
2 teaspoons lemon juice
2 tablespoons chopped fresh parsley
4 cups coarsely chopped fresh spinach
8 ounces salmon fillet
Lemon wedges

STEPS

1. Preheat oven to 400 F. Place salmon on a foil-lined baking sheet, skin side down. Sprinkle with lemon juice and Greek seasoning. Bake, for 17 minutes.
2. Meanwhile, in a small saucepan, combine, oil, quinoa, and broth; bring to a boil. Reduce heat; simmer, covered until liquid is absorbed and quinoa is tender for about 15 minutes.
3. To serve, break salmon into 1-in. pieces using a fork. Place tomatoes, spinach, quinoa, and salmon in a bowl. Add cheese, herbs, and pepper; toss gently to combine. Serve with lemon wedges.

NUTRITION FACTS

Per Serving:

Calories: 427kcal
Carbohydrates: 34g
Protein: 32g
Fat: 18g
Saturated Fat: 4g
Fiber: 6g
Cholesterol: 64mg
Sodium: 773mg

Classic Crab Cakes

PREPARATION
10 MIN

SERVES FOR
8 PEOPLE

INGREDIENTS

1/8 teaspoon hot pepper sauce
1/4 teaspoon pepper
1/3 cup each chopped celery, green pepper and onion
1 teaspoon prepared mustard
1 tablespoon seafood seasoning
1 tablespoon minced fresh parsley
1 teaspoon Worcestershire sauce
1 large egg, beaten
1 pound fresh or canned crabmeat, drained, flaked and cartilage removed
2 to 2-1/2 cups soft bread crumbs
2 teaspoons lemon juice
3/4 cup mayonnaise
4 tablespoons vegetable oil
Lemon wedges

STEPS

1. In a bowl, combine the crab, egg, bread crumbs, vegetables, mayonnaise, and seasonings. Shape into 8 patties. Cook patties in a cast-iron skillet in oil for 5 minutes on each side. Garnish with lemon.
2. Serve!

NUTRITION FACTS

Per Serving:

Calories: 282kcal
Carbohydrates: 7g
Protein: 14g
Fat: 22g
Saturated Fat: 3g
Fiber: 1g
Cholesterol: 85mg
Sodium: 638mg

Easy Crab Cakes

PREPARATION
5 MIN

SERVES FOR
4 PEOPLE

INGREDIENTS

1/8 teaspoon pepper
1/4 cup finely chopped sweet red pepper
1/4 cup reduced-fat mayonnaise
1/2 teaspoon garlic powder
1 tablespoon lemon juice
1 large egg, lightly beaten
1 tablespoon butter
1 cup seasoned bread crumbs, divided
2 green onions, finely chopped
2 cans (6 ounces each) crabmeat, drained, flaked and cartilage removed

STEPS

1. In a bowl, combine 1/3 cup bread crumbs, the egg, mayonnaise, red pepper, lemon juice, garlic powder, green onions, and pepper; fold in crab.
2. Place remaining bread crumbs in a shallow bowl. Divide mixture into eight portions; shape into 2-in. balls. Gently coat in bread crumbs and shape into 1/2-in.-thick patties.
3. In a nonstick skillet, heat butter over medium heat. Add crab balls; cook until golden brown, for about 4 minutes on each side. Serve!

NUTRITION FACTS

Per Serving:

Calories: 239kcal
Carbohydrates: 13g
Protein: 21g
Fat: 11g
Saturated Fat: 3g
Fiber: 1g
Cholesterol: 141mg
Sodium: 657mg

PREPARATION
20 MIN

SERVES FOR
24 APPETIZERS

Mini Crab Cakes

NUTRITION FACTS

Per Serving:
Calories: 134kcal; Carbohydrates: 3g; Protein: 4g; Fat: 12g; Saturated Fat: 1g; Cholesterol: 36mg;
Sodium: 402mg

INGREDIENTS

1/4 cup sour cream
1/4 teaspoon coarse salt
1/4 cup unsalted butter, melted, plus more for pans
1/2 teaspoon finely grated lemon peel
1 large egg
1 teaspoon finely grated orange peel
1 cup Japanese breadcrumbs
3/4 cup finely grated Parmesan cheese, divided
4 teaspoons plus 2 tablespoons chopped fresh chives, divided
6 ounces fresh lump crabmeat, picked over, patted dry, coarsely shredded
8 ounces cream cheese, room temperature
Large pinch of pepper
Fresh chives, cut into pieces

STEPS

1. Using an electric mixer, beat cream cheese in a bowl until smooth. Add 1/4 cup Parmesan and egg; beat to blend. Beat in sour cream, 4 teaspoons chopped chives, citrus peels coarse, salt, and pepper. Fold in crabmeat. Cover and chill.
2. Preheat oven to 375 degrees F. Generously butter 2 mini muffin pans. Toss panko, 1/2 cup Parmesan, and 2 tablespoons chopped chives in a bowl. Drizzle 1/4 cup melted butter over, tossing with fork until evenly moistened. Press 1 rounded tablespoon panko mixture into the bottom of each muffin cup, forming crust. Spoon 1 generous tablespoon of crab mixture into each cup. Sprinkle a rounded teaspoon of panko mixture over each.
3. Bake crab cakes, for about 30 minutes. Cool in pans for 5 minutes. Run a knife around each cake and gently lift it out of the pan. Arrange crab cakes on a serving platter; garnishwith chives. Serve!

Crab Stuffed Mushrooms

PREPARATION
15 MIN

SERVES FOR
4 PEOPLE

INGREDIENTS

1/3 cup mayonnaise
1 garlic clove, minced
2 tablespoons grated Parmesan cheese
3 tablespoons seasoned bread crumbs
6 ounces crabmeat, drained, flaked and carti-lage removed
18 medium fresh mushrooms
Minced fresh parsley

STEPS

1. Remove stems from mushrooms and set caps aside.
2. Mix mayonnaise, crab, cheese, bread crumbs, and garlic In a bowl.
3. Combine into mushroom caps.
4. Bake at 400 degrees F, cook for about 25 minutes. Garnish with parsley.
5. Serve!

NUTRITION FACTS

Per Serving:

Calories: 51kcal
Carbohydrates: 2g
Protein: 3g
Fat: 4g
Saturated Fat: 1.g
Fiber: 0g
Cholesterol: 10mg
Sodium: 81mg

Steamed Cod

PREPARATION
10 MIN

SERVES FOR
4 PEOPLE

INGREDIENTS

1/2 cup orange juice
1 tablespoon cornstarch
1 green onion, chopped
1 cup canned coconut milk
1 teaspoon soy sauce
1 teaspoon minced fresh gingerroot
11 ounces mandarin oranges, drained
1 tablespoon sesame oil
2 tablespoons sweet chili sauce
2 tablespoons sliced almonds
6 ounces cod fillets
Minced fresh cilantro

STEPS

1. In a saucepan, place a steamer basket over 1 in. of water. Place cod in the basket. Bring water to a boil. Reduce heat to maintain a low boil; steam, covered, for 12 minutes.
2. Meanwhile, in small saucepan whisk cornstarch, orange juice, and coconut milk until smooth. Add ginger, chili sauce, and soy sauce. Cook and stir over medium heat until thickened, for about 2 minutes. Stir in green onion, and sesame oil; heat through. Serve with cod; garnish with cilantro.
3. Serve!

NUTRITION FACTS

Per Serving:

Calories: 330kcal
Carbohydrates: 19g
Protein: 29g
Fat: 15g
Saturated Fat: 10g
Fiber: 1g
Cholesterol: 65mg
Sodium: 316mg

Tuna Burgers

PREPARATION
10 MIN

SERVES FOR
4 PEOPLE

INGREDIENTS

1/4 cup finely chopped onion
1/3 cup mayonnaise
1/2 cup dry bread crumbs
1/2 cup finely chopped celery
1 large egg, lightly beaten
2 tablespoons chili sauce
2 tablespoons butter
6.4 ounces light tuna in water
4 hamburger buns, split and toasted
Lettuce leaves and sliced tomato

STEPS

1. Mix the onion, bread crumbs, mayonnaise, celery, egg, tuna, and chili sauce. Shape into 4 patties.
2. In a cast-iron skillet, heat butter over medium heat. Cook patties until lightly browned, for 5 minutes on each side. Serve on buns. Garnish with lettuce and tomato.
3. Serve!

NUTRITION FACTS

Per Serving:

Calories: 417kcal
Carbohydrates: 35g
Protein: 17g
Fat:23g
Saturated Fat: 7g
Fiber: 2g
Cholesterol: 79mg
Sodium: 710mg

Asparagus Tuna Noodle Casserole

PREPARATION
20 MIN

SERVES FOR
8 PEOPLE

INGREDIENTS

1/4 cup lemon juice
1/2 teaspoon pepper
1/2 ounces condensed cream of asparagus soup, undiluted
1 medium sweet red pepper, chopped
1 small onion, chopped
1 teaspoon garlic salt
1 cup multigrain snack chips, crushed
1 tablespoon dried parsley flakes, divided
1-1/2 teaspoons smoked paprika, divided
1-1/2 cups shredded Colby cheese
2 cups uncooked elbow macaroni
2 cups sliced fresh mushrooms
2 pounds fresh asparagus, cut into 1-inch pieces
2 pouches (6.4 ounces each) light tuna in water
4 bacon strips, cooked and crumbled

STEPS

1. Cook macaroni according to package directions for al dente; drain. Transfer greased slow cooker and add in soup, onion, garlic, mushrooms, red pepper, lemon juice, 1-1/2 teaspoons parsley, 1 teaspoon paprika, salt, and pepper. Cook, covered, on low 3 hours.
2. Stir in asparagus and tuna. Cook, covered, on low until asparagus is crisp-tender, 1 hour longer. Sprinkle with remaining 1-1/2 teaspoons parsley and 1/2 teaspoon paprika. Serve with cheese, crushed chips, and bacon.

NUTRITION FACTS

Per Serving:

Calories: 338kcal
Carbohydrates: 30g
Protein: 22g
Fat: 15g
Saturated Fat: 6g
Fiber: 5g
Cholesterol: 44mg
Sodium: 1110mg

Tuna Mushroom Casserole

PREPARATION
30 MIN

SERVES FOR
6 PEOPLE

INGREDIENTS

1/8 teaspoon pepper
1/4 cup mayonnaise
1/4 cup chopped celery
1/3 cup dry bread crumbs
1/2 teaspoon dill weed
1/2 teaspoon salt
1/2 cup shredded Swiss cheese
1/2 cup water
1 teaspoon chicken bouillon granules
1 cup chopped onion
1 garlic clove, minced
1 cup sliced fresh mushrooms
1 tablespoon butter
1-1/2 cups cold whole milk
2-1/2 cups egg noodles, cooked and drained
4 teaspoons cornstarch
9 ounces frozen cut green beans
12 ounces light tuna in water, drained and flaked

NUTRITION FACTS

Per Serving:

Calories: 343kcal
Carbohydrates: 27g
Protein: 24g
Fat: 15g
Saturated Fat: 5g
Fiber: 2g
Cholesterol: 57mg
Sodium: 770mg

STEPS

1. In a saucepan, bring water and bouillon to a boil; stir until bouillon is dissolved. Add onion, celery, green beans, mushrooms, garlic, dill weed, salt, and pepper; bring to a boil. Reduce heat; cover and simmer until vegetables are tender, for 7 minutes.

2. In a bowl, combine cornstarch and milk until smooth; gradually add to vegetable mixture. Bring to a boil; cook and stir until thickened, about 3 minutes. Remove from the heat; stir in cheese and mayonnaise until cheese is melted. Fold in noodles and tuna.

3. Pour into a greased baking dish. In a small skillet, brown bread crumbs in butter; sprinkle over casserole. Bake, uncovered, at 375 degrees F until heated through, for 30 minutes. Serve!

Crunchy Tuna Wraps

PREPARATION
5 MIN

SERVES FOR
2 PEOPLE

INGREDIENTS

1 pouch (6.4 ounces) light tuna in water
1/4 cup finely chopped celery
1/4 cup chopped green onions
1/4 cup sliced water chestnuts, chopped
3 tablespoons chopped sweet red pepper
2 tablespoons reduced-fat mayonnaise
2 teaspoons prepared mustard
2 spinach tortillas, room temperature
1 cup shredded lettuce

STEPS

1. In a bowl, mix tuna, water chest-nuts, celery, green onions, sweet red pepper, mustard, and mayon-naise until blended. Spread over tortillas; sprinkle with lettuce. Roll up tightly and serve!

NUTRITION FACTS

Per Serving:

Calories: 312kcal
Carbohydrates: 34g
Protein: 23g
Fat: 10g
Saturated Fat: 2g
Fiber: 3g
Cholesterol: 38mg
Sodium: 628mg

Steamed Clams

PREPARATION
30 MIN

SERVES FOR
4 PEOPLE

INGREDIENTS

1/4 red pepper cored and chopped
1/3 cup chopped fresh parsley
1/2 teaspoon cumin
1/2 cup chopped red pepper
1/2 cup chopped green pepper
1/2 green pepper cored and chopped
1/2 tsp red pepper flakes
1/2 tsp smoked paprika
1 yellow onion chopped
1 cup dry white wine
1 green onion trimmed and chopped (both white and green parts)
1 1/2 cup water
2 ripe tomatoes chopped
3 pounds littleneck clams
4 garlic cloves minced
Salt and pepper
Extra virgin olive oil

NUTRITION FACTS

Per Serving:

Calories: 141.2kcal
Carbohydrates: 11.8g
Protein: 9.2g
Saturated Fat: 0.3g
Fiber: 2.3g

STEPS

1. Sort through clams and discard any already open ones that won't close.
2. Prepare three bowls, fill two of them with cool water and add a good amount of salt to each about 1/3 cup of salt to 1 gallon of water. Fill the third bowl with water but NO salt this time.
3. Clean the clams. Put the clams in the first bowl of cool salted water and set them aside for 30 minutes or so. Transfer the clams to the second bowl, making sure to discard any clams that are open and discard the dirty water from the first bowl. Set aside for another 30 minutes. Using a small brush, scrub the clams clean and transfer them to the last bowl of unsalted water. Allow them another 30 minutes. Transfer the clean clams to a tray and cover with a damp towel to keep them cool water and place the bowls in the fridge.
4. Make the white wine broth. In a pan heat 1/4 cup extra virgin olive oil over medium heat until shimmering but not smoking. Add the onions, garlic, and peppers. Season with salt and pepper and cook for 6 minutes, tossing regularly and making sure the garlic does

not burn.

5. Stir in the tomatoes and add the cumin, paprika, and red pepper flakes. Pour in the white wine and water. Raise the heat to bring the liquid to a gentle boil. Cook for a few minutes until the tomatoes soften for about 6 minutes. Add another pinch of salt.

6. Steam the clams in the white wine sauce. Lower the heat back to medium and add the clams. Cover with a lid and cook until the majority of the clams are open for 10 minutes. Discard any clams that are still closed.

7. Turn the heat off. Add the parsley, and green onion.

8. Serve immediately!

Modern Tuna Casserole

PREPARATION
20 MIN

SERVES FOR
6 PEOPLE

INGREDIENTS

1/4 teaspoon pepper
1/3 cup half-and-half cream
1/2 cup shredded Parmesan cheese
1 cup frozen peas
1 medium onion, chopped
1 medium sweet red pepper, chopped
1 tablespoon all-purpose flour
1 cup sliced baby portobello mushrooms
2 cups fresh baby spinach
2/3 cup reduced-sodium chicken broth
3 cups uncooked spiral pasta
3/4 teaspoon salt
3 tablespoons butter, divided
4 medium carrots, chopped
5 ounces albacore white tuna in water, drained
and flaked

STEPS

1. In a skillet, heat 1 tablespoon butter over medium heat. Add onion, carrots, red pepper, and mushrooms. Cook and stir, for 12 minutes. Add spinach, peas, and tuna; cook until spinach is just wilted, for about 3 minutes.

2. Meanwhile, cook pasta according to package directions. Drain pasta, reserving 1 cup pasta water. In a bowl, place pasta and tuna mixture; toss to combine. Wipe skillet clean.

3. In the same skillet, melt the remaining butter over medium heat. Stir in flour until smooth; gradually whisk in broth and cream. Bring to a boil, stirring constantly; cook and stir until thickened, 1-2 minutes, adding reserved pasta water if needed. Stir in cheese, salt, and pepper, and garnish pasta. Serve!

NUTRITION FACTS

Per Serving:

Calories: 372kcal
Carbohydrates: 44g
Protein: 23g
Fat: 11g
Saturated Fat: 6g
Cholesterol: 47mg
Sodium: 767mg

Mediterranean Tuna Salad

PREPARATION
15 MIN

SERVES FOR
4 PEOPLE

INGREDIENTS

1/4 teaspoon salt
1/4 teaspoon pepper
1/2 teaspoon dried basil
1/2 cup crumbled feta
1 small sweet red pepper, chopped
2 tablespoons olive oil
2 tablespoons balsamic vinegar
2 tablespoons spicy brown mustard
3 celery ribs, chopped
4 cups shredded lettuce
4 green onions, chopped
5 ounces albacore white tuna in water
15 ounces chickpeas, rinsed and drained

STEPS

1. In a bowl, combine the celery, beans, green onions, and red pepper. In an ather bowl, whisk the vinegar, oil, basil, mustard, salt, and pepper. Pour over bean mixture; toss to coat. Gently stir in tuna.
2. Serve over lettuce. Garnish with Feta cheese.

NUTRITION FACTS

Per Serving:

Calories: 282kcal
Carbohydrates: 23g
Protein: 23g
Fat: 11g
Fiber: 6g
Cholesterol: 30mg
Sodium: 682mg

Avocado Tuna Salad Sandwiches

PREPARATION
15 MIN

SERVES FOR
4 PEOPLE

INGREDIENTS

1/8 teaspoon pepper
1/4 teaspoon salt
1/3 cup mayonnaise
1 medium ripe avocado, peeled and sliced
2 pouches albacore white tuna in water
2 tablespoons lime juice
2 garlic cloves, minced
3 tablespoons minced fresh cilantro
4 slices Muenster
8 slices whole wheat bread

STEPS

1. In a bowl, mix the tuna, cilantro, garlic, mayonnaise, lime juice, salt, and pepper. Spread tuna mixture over 4 slices of bread; garnish with Muenster, avocado, and remaining bread.
2. Serve immediately!

NUTRITION FACTS

Per Serving:

Calories: 506kcal
Carbohydrates: 28g
Protein: 30g
Fat: 30g
Saturated Fat: 8g
Fiber: 6g
Cholesterol: 56mg
Sodium: 908mg

Tuna and White Bean Lettuce Wraps

PREPARATION
5 MIN

SERVES FOR
6 PEOPLE

INGREDIENTS

1/8 teaspoon salt
1/8 teaspoon pepper
1/4 cup chopped red onion
1 medium ripe avocado, peeled and sliced
1 tablespoon minced fresh parsley
2 tablespoons olive oil
12 lettuce leaves
12 ounces light tuna in water, drained and flaked
15 ounces cannellini beans, rinsed and drained

STEPS

1. In a bowl, combine the tuna, red onion, olive oil, beans, parsley, salt, and pepper; toss lightly to combine. Serve in lettuce leaves; garnish with avocado. Serve!

NUTRITION FACTS

Per Serving:

Calories: 279kcal
Carbohydrates: 19g
Protein: 22g
Fat: 13g
Saturated Fat: 2g
Fiber: 7g
Cholesterol: 31mg
Sodium: 421mg

Lobster Bisque

PREPARATION
35 MIN

SERVES FOR
2 PEOPLE

INGREDIENTS

1 medium onion, chopped
1 teaspoon minced fresh thyme
1 teaspoon coarsely ground pepper
1-1/2 teaspoons salt
2 cups heavy whipping cream
2 live lobsters
2 medium carrots, peeled and chopped
3 tablespoons butter
2 tablespoons tomato paste
2 garlic cloves, minced
2/3 cup uncooked long grain rice
3/4 cup white wine or sherry
32 ounces seafood stock
Minced fresh parsley

NUTRITION FACTS

Per Serving:

373 calories
protein 10g
carbohydrates 20g
fat 26g
cholesterol 127mg
sodium 942mg

STEPS

1. In a Dutch oven, add 2 inches of water; bring to a rolling boil. Add lobsters, cover, and steam for 9 minutes. Remove lobsters, reserving liquid. When cool enough to handle, remove meat from claws and tail, reserving any juices; refrigerate meat and juices.
2. In the same Dutch oven, cook onion, and carrots in butter over medium heat, for 7 minutes. Stir in tomato paste and cook until it starts to caramelize for about 6 minutes. Add garlic; cook for 1 minute. Stir in wine and simmer until reduced by half. Add lobster shells, bodies, reserved cooking liquid, reserved lobster juices, and stock. Bring mixture to a simmer; cook for 1 hour. Strain mixture, pressing to extract as much liquid as possible; discard shells and solids.
3. Put back liquid into Dutch oven. Add rice and cook until extremely soft, for 35 minutes. Puree in a blender until smooth. Add thyme, cream, salt, and pepper. Bring mixture to a very low simmer; add reserved lobster meat and cook until heated through. Garnish with black pepper and parsley. Serve!

Traditional New England Clam Chowder

SEAFOOD

PREPARATION
40 MIN

SERVES FOR
6 PEOPLE

INGREDIENTS

1/4 teaspoon pepper
1/4 teaspoon salt
1/2 cup half-and-half cream
1 cup whole milk
1 small onion, chopped
2 bacon strips, diced
2 medium potatoes, peeled and finely chopped
2 tablespoons all-purpose flour
3 cups cold water
12 fresh cherrystone clams

STEPS

1. Tap clams; discard any that do not close. Place clams and water in a saucepan. Bring to a boil. Reduce heat; cover and simmer for 7 minutes.
2. Remove meat from clams; chop meat and set aside. Strain liquid through a cheesecloth-lined colander; set aside.
3. In another saucepan, cook bacon over medium heat until crisp. Using a slotted spoon, remove a paper towel. Saute onion.
4. Return bacon to the pan; add clam meat and reserved liquid. Stir in the potatoes, salt, and pepper. Bring to a boil. Reduce heat; cover and simmer for 15 minutes.
5. Combine flour and milk until smooth; gradually stir into soup. Bring to a boil; cook and stir for 3 minutes. Gradually stir in cream; mix for about 1 minute. Serve!

NUTRITION FACTS

Per Serving:
Calories: 138kcal
Carbohydrates: 14g
Protein: 6g
Fat: 6g
Saturated Fat: 3g
Fiber: 1g
Cholesterol: 24mg
Sodium: 175mg

Linguine with Herbed Clam Sauce

PREPARATION
20 MIN

SERVES FOR
4 PEOPLE

INGREDIENTS

1/4 cup olive oil
1/4 cup butter
1/4 cup minced fresh basil
1/3 cup minced fresh parsley
1/2 cup finely chopped onion
1/2 cup white wine
2 tablespoons cornstarch
4 garlic cloves, minced
6-1/2 ounces minced clams
10 ounces whole baby clams
Dash pepper
Dash cayenne pepper
Hot cooked linguine
Shredded Parmesan cheese

STEPS

1. Drain baby and minced clams, reserving juice; set clams and juice aside. In a skillet, saute onion in oil and butter until tender. Add parsley and garlic; saute for 1 minute.
2. Add drained clams; saute 2 minutes longer.
3. Combine cornstarch and clam juice until smooth; stir into skillet with wine. Bring to a boil; cook and stir for 2 minutes. Stir in the basil, pepper, and cayenne. Serve sauce over linguine; garnish with Parmesan cheese.
4. Serve!

NUTRITION FACTS

Per Serving:

Calories: 328kcal
Carbohydrates: 10g
Protein: 10g
Fat: 26g
Saturated Fat: 9g
Cholesterol: 73mg
Sodium: 521mg

Slow-Cooker Clam Sauce

PREPARATION
10 MIN

SERVES FOR
4 PEOPLE

INGREDIENTS

1/4 teaspoon white pepper
1/4 teaspoon black pepper
1/4 teaspoon Italian seasoning
1/4 cup sherry
1/2 teaspoon garlic salt
1/2 cup finely chopped onion
1/2 cup water
1 bay leaf
2 tablespoons olive oil
2 teaspoons lemon juice
2 tablespoons chopped fresh parsley
2 garlic cloves, minced
3/4 teaspoon dried oregano
4 tablespoons butter
8 ounces fresh mushrooms, chopped
10 ounces whole baby clams
Hot cooked pasta
Grated Parmesan cheese

STEPS

1. Heat butter and oil in a skillet over medium heat. Add onion; cook and stir for 4 minutes. Add mushrooms and garlic; cook for 6 minutes more.

2. Drain clams, reserving liquid; coarsely chop. Place clams, reserved clam juice, mushroom mixture, garlic, bay leaf, oregano, Italian seasoning, sherry, white pepper, and black pepper in the water 5-qt. a slow cooker. Cook, covered, on low for about 2 hours. Remove and discard bay leaf; stir in parsley. Serve with pasta. Garnish with Parmesan cheese and fresh parsley.

NUTRITION FACTS

Per Serving:

Calories: 138kcal
Carbohydrates: 5g
Protein: 7g
Fat: 10g
Saturated Fat: 4g
Fiber: 0g
Cholesterol: 40mg
Sodium: 580mg

Instant Pot Clam Chowder

PREPARATION
20 MIN

SERVES FOR
8 PEOPLE

INGREDIENTS

1/2 teaspoon pepper
1 cup heavy whipping cream
1 cup chicken broth
1 teaspoon dried thyme
1 teaspoon salt
1 medium onion, chopped
8 ounces clam juice
2 tablespoons all-purpose flour
2 celery ribs, chopped
2 medium carrots, chopped
4 garlic cloves, minced
4 medium potatoes, peeled and cut into 1/2-inch cubes
4 bacon strips, cooked and crumbled
6-1/2 ounces minced clams, undrained
Fresh thyme

STEPS

1. Place the onion, carrots, potatoes, celery ribs, clam juice, chicken broth, dried thyme, salt, and pepper in a 6-qt. electric pressure cooker. Drain and reserve liquid from clams; add the liquid to the pressure cooker and set clams aside. Lock lid; close pressure-release valve. Adjust to pressure-cook on high for 14 minutes. Quick-release pressure.
2. Select saute setting and adjust for low heat. Mix flour and cream until smooth; add into the soup. Cook and stir until slightly thickened, for 7 minutes. Stir in clams; heat through. Garnish with bacon and, fresh thyme. Serve!

NUTRITION FACTS

Per Serving:

Calories: 227kcal
Carbohydrates: 21g
Protein: 8g
Fat: 13g
Saturated Fat: 7g
Fiber: 1.4g
Cholesterol: 56mg
Sodium: 673mg

Avocado Crab Boats

PREPARATION
20 MIN

SERVES FOR
8 PEOPLE

INGREDIENTS

1/4 teaspoon pepper
1/2 teaspoon paprika
1/2 cup mayonnaise
1 serrano pepper, seeded and minced
1 tablespoon capers, drained
1 cup shredded pepper jack cheese
2 tablespoons lemon juice
2 tablespoons minced chives
4 tablespoons chopped fresh cilantro, divided
5 medium ripe avocados, peeled and halved
6 ounces lump crabmeat, drained
Lemon wedges

STEPS

1. Preheat broiler. Place 2 avocado halves in a bowl; mash lightly with a fork. Add lemon juice, mayonnaise, and mix until well blended. Stir in crab, 3 tablespoons cilantro, serrano pepper, chives capers, and pepper. Spoon into remaining avocado halves.

2. Transfer to a baking pan. Sprinkle with cheese and paprika. Broil 4-5 in. from heat until cheese is melted, 3-5 minutes. Garnish with remaining cilantro; serve with lemon wedges.

NUTRITION FACTS

Per Serving:

Calories: 325kcal
Carbohydrates : 8 g
Protein: 13g
Fat: 28g
Saturated fat: 6g
Cholesterol: 57mg
Sodium: 427mg

Sweet Potato and Crab Soup

PREPARATION
15 MIN

SERVES FOR
8 PEOPLE

INGREDIENTS

1/2 teaspoon ground cinnamon
1/2 teaspoon pepper
1 teaspoon salt, divided
2 cups heavy whipping cream
2 medium leeks (white portion only), finely chopped
3 garlic cloves, minced
4 teaspoons fresh thyme leaves, divided
4 tablespoons butter, divided
4 cups cubed peeled sweet potatoes
5 cups vegetable stock
12 ounces lump crabmeat, drained
Croutons

STEPS

1. In a Dutch oven, heat 2 tablespoons butter over medium heat; saute leeks and garlic, for 5 minutes.
2. Stir in sweet potatoes, cinnamon, 3/4 teaspoon salt, pepper, and stock; bring to a boil. Reduce heat; simmer, covered, for 20 minutes.
3. Puree soup using an immersion blender and puree soup in batches in a blender; return to pan. Stir in cream and 2 teaspoons thyme; bring to a boil. Reduce heat; simmer, uncovered, 6 minutes.
4. Meanwhile, in a skillet, melt the remaining butter over low. Add crab and the remaining salt and thyme; cook 5 minutes, stirring gently to combine. Garnish servings with crab mixture and croutons.
5. Serve!

NUTRITION FACTS

Per Serving:

Calories: 370kcal
Carbohydrates: 20g
Protein: 11g
Fat: 28g
Saturated Fat: 18g
Fiber: 3g
Cholesterol: 124mg
Sodium: 994mg

Red Clam Sauce

PREPARATION
25 MIN

SERVES FOR
4 PEOPLE

INGREDIENTS

1/4 cup minced fresh parsley
1/2 teaspoon dried thyme
1 bay leaf
1 teaspoon sugar
1 teaspoon dried basil
1 medium onion, chopped
1 tablespoon canola oil
2 garlic cloves, minced
6 ounces tomato paste
6 ounces linguine, cooked and drained
6-1/2 ounces chopped clams, undrained
14-1/2 ounces diced tomatoes, undrained
Additional minced fresh parsley

STEPS

1. In a skillet, saute onion in oil, for 3 minutes. Add garlic; cook 1 minute longer.
2. Transfer to a 1-1/2- or 2-qt. slow cooker. Stir in tomatoes, tomato paste, sugar, clams, parsley, bay leaf, basil, and thyme.
3. Cover and cook on low for about 3 hours. Discard bay leaf. Garnish with parsley. Serve with linguine.

NUTRITION FACTS

Per Serving:

Calories: 305kcal
Carbohydrates: 53g
Protein: 15g
Fat: 5g
Saturated Fat: 0g
Fiber: 7g
Cholesterol: 15mg
Sodium: 553mg